Palgrave Studies in Political Marketing and Management

Series Editor
Jennifer Lees-Marshment
School of Social Science,
Politics and International Relations
University of Auckland
Auckland, New Zealand

Palgrave Studies in Political Marketing and Management (PalPMM) series publishes high quality and ground-breaking academic research on this growing area of government and political behaviour that attracts increasing attention from scholarship, teachers, the media and the public. It covers political marketing intelligence including polling, focus groups, role play, co-creation, segmentation, voter profiling, stakeholder insight; the political consumer; political management including crisis management, change management, issues management, reputation management, delivery management; political advising; political strategy such as positioning, targeting, market-orientation, political branding; political leadership in all its many different forms and arena; political organization including managing a political office, political HR, internal party marketing; political communication management such as public relations and e-marketing and ethics of political marketing and management.

For more information email the series editor Jennifer Lees-Marshment on j.lees-marshment@auckland.ac.nz and see https://leesmarshment.wordpress.com/pmm-book-series/.

Andrew Lim

Political Marketing and Public Diplomacy by Pro-Israel and Pro-Palestinian Advocacy Groups

Andrew Lim
Politics and International Relations
University of Auckland
Auckland, New Zealand

Palgrave Studies in Political Marketing and Management
ISBN 978-3-031-15331-0   ISBN 978-3-031-15332-7   (eBook)
https://doi.org/10.1007/978-3-031-15332-7

© The Author(s), under exclusive licence to Springer Nature Switzerland AG 2022
This work is subject to copyright. All rights are solely and exclusively licensed by the Publisher, whether the whole or part of the material is concerned, specifically the rights of translation, reprinting, reuse of illustrations, recitation, broadcasting, reproduction on microfilms or in any other physical way, and transmission or information storage and retrieval, electronic adaptation, computer software, or by similar or dissimilar methodology now known or hereafter developed.
The use of general descriptive names, registered names, trademarks, service marks, etc. in this publication does not imply, even in the absence of a specific statement, that such names are exempt from the relevant protective laws and regulations and therefore free for general use.
The publisher, the authors, and the editors are safe to assume that the advice and information in this book are believed to be true and accurate at the date of publication. Neither the publisher nor the authors or the editors give a warranty, expressed or implied, with respect to the material contained herein or for any errors or omissions that may have been made. The publisher remains neutral with regard to jurisdictional claims in published maps and institutional affiliations.

This Palgrave Macmillan imprint is published by the registered company Springer Nature Switzerland AG.
The registered company address is: Gewerbestrasse 11, 6330 Cham, Switzerland

This book is dedicated to my father Jimmy Lim Chee Peng, 1957–2022.

Acknowledgements

This book is derived from my PhD research, which examined how advocacy groups in New Zealand and Australia conducted political marketing and nation branding in support of both Israeli and Palestinian public diplomacy initiatives. This book would not have been possible without the support of everyone including my former doctoral supervisor Dr Jennifer Lees-Marshment, the Palgrave Macmillan editorial team, University of Auckland staff members, fellow PhD students, research participants, family members, and friends. I appreciate the guidance, support, and sense of community that they all provided.

First, I would like to thank my former supervisor Dr Jennifer Lees-Marshment, who is also the series editor for Palgrave Macmillan's Political Marketing and Management series. Besides shepherding me throughout the PhD process, particularly the development of the analytical framework and methodology, Lees-Marshment encouraged me to adapt my PhD research into a book. I would also like to thank my Palgrave editors particularly Karthika Devi Ravikumar, Anne-Kathrin Birchley-Brun, Rebecca Roberts, and Kiruthika Counassegarane for taking the time to respond to my numerous queries during the writing and editing phase.

Second, I would like to thank the other University of Auckland staff who were involved in my PhD research at a professional level. As co-supervisor, Dr Geoff Kemp provided useful advice and served as a second "pair of eyes." In addition, I am grateful to Learning Adviser Jackie Ede for providing invaluable support and advice throughout the data collection and writing stages of my PhD research. I also appreciated her patience and kindness. I would also like to acknowledge my initial supervision team Dr Stephen Hoadley and Dr Thomas Gregory, who guided me in the initial stage.

Third, I would like to thank my fellow PhD students particularly Salma Malik, Joyce Manyo, Jordan Hanford, Hasith Eranda, and Latiff K.M. Haneefa for providing critical advice and feedback throughout the PhD journey. Joyce taught me a lot about critical case sampling while Salma and Hasith assisted me with various Facebook extraction software including Netvizz. Jordan and Latiff also took a genuine interest in my PhD research, asking hard questions and providing feedback. I would also like to thank Luna Zhao, Bey Widodo, Fung Chan, and Warit Chanprasert for listening to my countless presentations and teaching me about Zoom.

Fourth, I would like to thank all my research participants who agreed to spare the time to be interviewed for this research. John Minto, Dr David Cumin, and Jessica Morrison provided critical information about their organisations which helped to fill research gaps. I would also like to thank my initial research participants Ambassador Izzat Salah Abdulhadi, Roger Fowler, Juliet Moses, Janfrie Wakim, Leslie Bravery, Stephanie and Taiawa Harawira, Derek McDowell, and Tony Kan. While their input did not make the final cut of the PhD research, they were used to inform early thinking and development of the research focus and framework.

Fifth, I would like to thank my parents Jimmy Lim and Ooi Tong Siew for providing financial and moral support during my university years. While my father did not live to see me graduate, I am grateful for his support and have dedicated this book to his memory. I am also grateful to my brothers David and Peter for encouraging me along the way.

Finally, I would like to thank my friends who encouraged me throughout the PhD process including my Israeli penfriend Daveed Shachar, my spiritual families at St Andrew's First Presbyterian, Musselburgh Baptist churches and the Student Life Christian club, and Ian Howard, who taught me chess. Sylvia Wheeldon, Renu Jabin, and Maritza Kloppers helped provide a safe living and learning environment during my five years at Carlaw Park Student Village. Last but not least, praise God for making the impossible possible.

Contents

1	Introduction	1
2	Palestine Solidarity Network Aotearoa	21
3	Israel Institute of New Zealand	45
4	Australia/Israel & Jewish Affairs Council	67
5	Australia Palestine Advocacy Network	97
6	Conclusion	121
Appendix		143
Index		145

About the Author

Andrew Lim completed his PhD at the University of Auckland, New Zealand, in 2021. His research examined the role of advocacy groups in supporting Israeli and Palestinian public diplomacy activities in New Zealand and Australia. The author previously studied at the University of Otago in New Zealand, graduating with a combined BA Honours in History and Political Studies in 2014 and completing an MA in History in 2015. Lim's MA research looked at New Zealand foreign policy towards Indonesia during the Sukarno period between 1945 and 1966. The author's published works have included an article in the *New Zealand Journal of Asian Studies* looking at New Zealand media coverage of the Indonesian-Malaysian Confrontation (1963–1966) and a co-authored chapter about pro-Israel and pro-Palestinian advocacy groups in New Zealand and Australia within *The Palgrave Encyclopedia of Interest Groups, Lobbying and Public Affairs*. Lim is also interested in New Zealand politics, history, and social issues.

Abbreviations

ABC	Australian Broadcasting Corporation
AFOPA	Australian Friends of Palestine Association
AIJAC	Australia/Israel and Jewish Affairs Council
AIR	*Australia/Israel Review*
AJC	American Jewish Committee
AJDS	Australian Jewish Democratic Society
AJN	*Australian Jewish News*
ALP	Australian Labor Party
APAN	Australia Palestine Advocacy Network
ASPI	Australian Strategic Policy Institute
AUJS	Australasian Union of Jewish Students
BDS	Boycott, Divestment, and Sanctions movement
BESA	Begin-Sadat Center for Strategic Studies
C4Israel	Christians for Israel New Zealand
ECAJ	Executive Council of Australian Jewry
GP&J	Global Peace and Justice
IDF	Israel Defense Forces
IHRA	International Holocaust Remembrance Alliance
IINZ	Israel Institute of New Zealand
ISO	International Socialist Organisation
J-AIR	Jewish-Australian Internet Radio
MEF	Middle East Forum
MFAT	Ministry of Foreign Affairs and Trade (New Zealand)
NPA	National Party of Australia
NZCTU	New Zealand Council of Trade Unions
NZJC	New Zealand Jewish Council

NZPSN	New Zealand Palestine Solidarity Network (predecessor to the PSNA)
PHRC	Palestine Human Rights Campaign
PLO	Palestinian Liberation Organisation
PSNA	Palestine Solidarity Network Aotearoa
SBS	Special Broadcasting Service
SJP	Students for Justice in Palestine
TVNZ	Television New Zealand
UIA	United Israel Appeal
UN	United Nations
UNSC	United Nations Security Council
UNESCO	United Nations Educational, Scientific, and Cultural Organization
WPG	Wellington Palestine Group
ZFNZ	Zionist Federation of New Zealand

List of Tables

Table 1.1	A model of how advocacy groups can use political marketing to support the public diplomacy and nation branding efforts of the Israeli and the Palestinian governments	8
Table 1.2	Tally of primary sources	11
Table 2.1	The PSNA analysed using Lees-Marshment's product-oriented framework	24
Table 2.2	Outline of field note observations from PSNA public meetings and speaking engagements	25
Table 3.1	The IINZ analysed using Lees-Marshment's sales-oriented framework	47
Table 4.1	AIJAC analysed using Lees-Marshment's sales-oriented framework	69
Table 5.1	APAN analysed using Lees-Marshment's product-oriented framework	99
Table 6.1	Did the advocacy groups adhere to the framework's criteria?	126

CHAPTER 1

Introduction

Abstract This chapter introduces the research topic: namely how advocacy groups can use political marketing to support the public diplomacy and nation branding efforts of the Israeli and the Palestinian governments. It also discusses the gaps within the academic literature on advocacy, political marketing, public diplomacy, and nation branding that this research intends to fill. The introduction also outlines the author's synthesised analytical framework, which draws upon theories and concepts from political marketing, public diplomacy, nation branding, and advocacy. This chapter also discusses the methodology and case studies before concluding with an outline of the book's chapters and contents.

Keywords Israel • Palestine • Advocacy • Political marketing • Public diplomacy • Nation branding

BACKGROUND

On September 28, 2015, two Israeli soldiers visited Victoria University of Wellington to deliver a lecture on the 2014 Operation Protective Edge sponsored by the Australasian Union of Jewish Students (AUJS). Their visit attracted a vigorous protest by members of the local Students for

© The Author(s), under exclusive license to Springer Nature Switzerland AG 2022
A. Lim, *Political Marketing and Public Diplomacy by Pro-Israel and Pro-Palestinian Advocacy Groups*, Palgrave Studies in Political Marketing and Management,
https://doi.org/10.1007/978-3-031-15332-7_1

Justice in Palestine (SJP), a Palestinian solidarity group that has adopted the global Boycott, Divestment, and Sanctions (BDS) campaign, which seeks to advance Palestinian rights and self-determination by applying economic and social pressure on Israel. In addition, 11 academics criticised the university for sponsoring an event which they regarded as "part of a nationwide campaign to justify Israel's latest war crimes in Gaza." The visit and resulting protest also attracted notable media coverage (Faitaua, 2015; Hunt, 2015). Besides reflecting the significant international controversy around Israel-Palestine issues, the incident demonstrated the competing efforts by various governments and non-state actors including advocacy groups to shape public opinion towards Israel and the Palestinians through public diplomacy, nation branding, and political marketing. While the Israeli Government and international pro-Israel advocacy groups have sought to promote a favourable image of Israeli resilience and self-defence, the Palestinian National Authority (PA) and Palestinian solidarity groups have sought to mobilise international support for the Palestinian cause and hold Israel accountable for alleged human rights abuses and aggression against the Palestinians.

Drawing upon the author's PhD research, this book will focus on how political marketing can be used outside of party politics and elections by various actors including advocacy groups, with specific attention to Zionist and Palestinian advocacy groups in New Zealand and Australia. It also explores how advocacy groups can support the public diplomacy and nation branding activities of states, focusing on the Israel-Palestine conflict. Besides expanding and updating the literature on both Zionist and Palestinian advocacy groups in New Zealand, it also contributes to the literature on Australian Palestinian advocacy groups by analysing the communications output and advocacy work of the Australia Palestine Advocacy Network (APAN), the national umbrella organisation there. In short, this book looks at the intersection between political marketing, advocacy, public diplomacy, and nation branding.

New Zealand and Australia were selected due to their cultural, political, and demographic similarities as well as their divergent foreign policy approaches towards Israel-Palestine. Both are former British settler colonies which have developed into wealthy liberal democracies with free market economies. Due to their history of colonisation, both countries have significant indigenous populations (namely the Māori in New Zealand, and the Australian Aborigines, and Torres Straits Islanders). As immigrant-receiving countries, both are home to significant Jewish and Arab diaspora populations. While New Zealand and Australian foreign policies have traditionally focused on the Asia-Pacific region, both states have followed developments in Israel-Palestine through the United Nations and other international bodies. Despite their stated support for a two-state solution, there are key differences in Wellington and Canberra's foreign policies towards Israel and the Palestinians. Whereas Australia has been a vocal supporter of Israel on the international stage, New Zealand has taken a more "even handed" position towards Israel and the Palestinians, criticising Israeli settlement expansion and violence on both sides (Badder, 2014; Han & Rane, 2013; Macintyre, 1986; Matthews & Arvanitakis, 2015; Reich, 2002; Rubenstein & Fleischer, 2007; Van Voorthuysen, 2011).

For example, New Zealand's co-sponsorship of United Nations Security Council (UNSC) Resolution 2334 in December 2016 strained bilateral relations with Israel. By contrast, Canberra criticised Resolution 2334 and subsequently hosted Israeli Prime Minister Benjamin Netanyahu in 2017 (Greene, 2016; Radio New Zealand, 2017; Stuff, 2016). While both Wellington and Canberra maintain diplomatic relations with Israel and unofficial relations with the Palestinian Authority, only Australia maintains an embassy (https://israel.embassy.gov.au/) in Tel Aviv and a representative office (https://ramallah.mission.gov.au/) in Ramallah. By contrast, New Zealand has no diplomatic presence in Israel-Palestine at the time of writing; instead accrediting its embassies in Turkey and Egypt to managing relations with Israel and the Palestinian Authority respectively (MFAT, n.d.). This is the cultural, political, and diplomatic environment that the Zionist and Palestinian solidarity groups in both Australia and New Zealand operate within.

Prior Literature

This book drew upon a range of academic literature from the advocacy, public diplomacy, nation branding, and political marketing fields. In terms of advocacy, the author's understanding of advocacy groups was informed by Keck and Sikkink's (1998) "transnational advocacy network," "political actions," and "boomerang pattern" models and Lang and Lang's (1983) and Cobb and Elder's (1972) research into agenda building. This book also reviewed the literature on advocacy groups in New Zealand and Australia. Most of the existing New Zealand literature on Israel-Palestine has focused on bilateral relations and trade while relegating advocacy groups to the margins (Macintyre, 1986, 1987; Rainbow, 1997; Ritchie,

1986; Van Voorthuysen, 2011). While Badder (2014) and Trotter (2019) have examined both historical and contemporary Jewish and Zionist groups in New Zealand, there was no exploration of the political marketing, public diplomacy, and nation branding dimensions of their advocacy activities. While there is a significant body of literature on Jewish and Zionist groups in Australia (Ben-Moshe, 2004; Han & Rane, 2013; Levey, 2004; Levey & Mendes, 2004; Loewenstein, 2006; Markus, 2004; Mendes, 2016; Reich, 2004; Rutland, 2004), there is comparatively limited research on Australian-based Palestinian groups (Mendes, 2006, 2016; Mendes & Dyrenfurth, 2015). As with the New Zealand literature, there was little exploration of the Australian groups' political marketing, public diplomacy, and nation branding activities.

In addition, the author surveyed the prior literature on overseas Zionist and Palestinian advocacy groups conducted by Mearsheimer and Walt (2007), Bard (2010), Hafsa (2014), Paul and Paul (2009), Miller (2004), Louvet (2016), Voltolini (2016), and King (2016). The author also consulted the literature on the Boycott, Divestment, and Sanctions (BDS) movement including Hallward (2013), Barnes (2014), Mendes and Dyrenfurth (2015), Matthews and Arvanitakis (2015), and Hitchcock (2016). The BDS movement is a loosely organised global civil society network seeking to advance Palestinian rights and self-determination by targeting Israel's economy, civil society, and international engagement. While the BDS National Committee in Ramallah serves as a Palestinian "reference point" for coordinating the BDS network, it does not direct the movement with international affiliates wielding considerable autonomy (Barnes, 2014; Hallward, 2013). The BDS campaign has been adopted by various Palestinian solidarity groups including those based in New Zealand and Australia. This international literature on Zionist and Palestinian advocacy groups as well as the BDS movement helps provide an international context to the transnational advocacy networks that embeds the New Zealand and Australian groups.

In terms of political marketing, the author consulted Lees-Marshment's (2001, 2003, 2004, 2014) "product/sales/market-oriented framework" and communications and relational activities; Bannon's (2004) and Ahuvia's (2012) ideas and concepts about segmentation; Lees-Marshment's (2014; Lees-Marshment et al., 2018) ideas about targeting; Bartle and Griffith's (Bartle & Griffiths, 2002) segmentation, targeting, and positioning (STP) process; and Pettitt's (2015) internal marketing framework. While there is a small body of political-marketing literature on the Arab-Israeli conflict and Israeli politics, none of them look at advocacy groups that advocate on Israel-Palestine issues. Astorino-Courtois (1996, 2000) has explored the use of political marketing to promote support for the peace process in Jordan, Israel, and the Palestinian Territories through public opinion surveys. Within the Israeli literature, Schonker-Schreck (2004), Auerbach and Yehuda (2010), Balmas and Sheafer (2010), and Orkibi (2015) have researched Israeli candidate branding, political communications, and election campaigning. There was also a lack of extensive prior research into Palestinian political marketing apart from Mozes and Weizmann's (2010) and Schleifer's (2014) research into Hamas' online political communications output. Unlike Israel, there has been no political marketing research conducted on Palestinian parties, politicians, and political institutions. There is also limited research on the political marketing of pro-Israel and pro-Palestinian advocacy groups apart from Lawrence's (2015) case study on the Inner West Jewish Community and Friends Peace Alliance's (iwJAFA) efforts to mobilise opposition against the Marrickville City Council's 2010 endorsement of the BDS campaign. By analysing the advocacy work of pro-Israel and pro-Palestinian groups from a political marketing angle, this book can help break new ground within the political marketing literature.

In terms of public diplomacy, the most useful models and concepts were Cull's (2009) "New Public Diplomacy" model, Gilboa's (2001, 2008) "non-state transnational model," and Zaharna's (2009) information and relational frameworks. One unresolved issue that Cull identified was the relationship between the output of these new actors and state interests. This raises the question of whether advocacy groups are unpaid auxiliaries of official public diplomacy efforts or whether they are independent actors with their own interests and agenda? The author consulted the substantial literature on Israeli public diplomacy including the scholarship of Cummings (2016), Gilboa (2001, 2006, 2008); Greenfield and Rothman (2012), Hadari and Turgeman (2016), Shai (2018), Toledano (2005, 2010), and Toledano and McKie (2009, 2013). One useful "boundary-spanning" work was Burla's (2015) case study on how the Israeli Government worked with community organisations to mobilise Australian Jewish diaspora support for Israel during the 2010 Gaza Flotilla incident; demonstrating that advocacy groups can support official public diplomacy efforts. There was also a limited body of literature on Palestinian public diplomacy by Zaharna (2003), Awad (2015), and Zaharna et al. (2009); which mainly focused on the Palestinian Authority's official public diplomacy but neglected the role of advocacy groups. The limited research conducted on Palestinian public diplomacy presents opportunities for further academic research in this area.

In terms of nation branding, the author surveyed the scholarship of Ollins (2002), van Ham (2001), Nimijean (2005, 2006), Gilboa (2008), Szondi (2008), Smits and Jensen (2012), Rockower (2012), Pamment (2013), and Dinnie (2016). The author identified a significant body of nation branding literature on Israel-Palestine issues including Brin's (2006) research into the role of advocacy groups in Israeli and Palestinian solidarity tourism in Jerusalem; Beirman's (2000, 2002) research into private-public nation branding partnerships in Australia; Campo and Alvarez's (2014) research into Israeli tourism marketing in Spain and Turkey; Avraham's (2009), Schulman's (2012), and Shai's (2018) research into the tourism and marketing dimensions of the Israeli Government's Brand Israel campaign; and Sahhar's discussion of the Australian and Israeli use of commemorative events to promote nationalism and militarism (2015). While there was a significant body of literature on Israeli official and informal Jewish nation branding activities, there was a lack of literature on Palestinian nation branding apart from Brin's (2006) research into informal Palestinian advocacy groups' solidarity tourism activities.

Research Question and Hypothesis

Based on the gaps identified in the literature review, this book seeks to address this research question: how do advocacy groups in New Zealand and Australia use political marketing to support the public diplomacy and nation branding efforts of the Israeli and the Palestinian governments?

The author also seeks to address the hypothesis that these advocacy groups are independent allies who support the public diplomacy and nation branding efforts of state actors through their communications output and advocacy activities. The null hypothesis is that the advocacy groups are proxies created by foreign governments to advance their public diplomacy and nation branding efforts through their communications output and advocacy activities. In short, this book intends to address the place of advocacy groups in political marketing, public diplomacy, and nation branding.

Theoretical Framework

To address the research question and hypothesis, the author proposes a new framework (as outlined in Table 1.1) that synthesises the fields of advocacy, political marketing, public diplomacy, and nation branding. The marketing orientation, "segmentation, targeting, and positioning," and internal marketing sections were influenced by Lees-Marshment's "product/sales/market-oriented framework," Bartle and Griffith's STP process, and Pettitt's internal marketing framework respectively. Table 1.1 is a condensed version of the synthesised analytical framework which the author developed in his PhD research, which this book draws upon. While the previous framework also looked at the groups' communications output, political communication, image management, relational activities, lobbying, networking, and fundraising, this condensed framework focuses more on their political marketing, public diplomacy, and nation branding activities.

Methodology

This research uses a qualitative methodological research design that was informed by a constructivist worldview and deductive approach. Taking a comparative case studies approach, this research also used two qualitative research methods: content analysis and elite interviews with representatives of the advocacy groups studied. Constructivism takes the premise that individuals make sense of the world through their social interactions and the influence of historical and cultural norms and forces (Creswell, 2009; Lincoln & Guba, 1985; Sarantakos, 2005). Due to the diametrically opposed Israeli and Palestinian positions, a constructivist framework provided the best explanation for how the two sides constructed meaning by promoting messages and arguments which supported their causes and narratives about Israel-Palestine. While pro-Israel advocates see themselves as defending the legitimacy and historical claims of Israel and the Jewish people against anti-Semitism, pro-Palestinian advocates view themselves as standing for Palestinian rights and self-determination against Zionist "settler colonialism." Taking a deductive approach, this research used the synthesised analytical framework outlined above to analyse a range of online, print, and audio-visual sources against the criteria of the research question, hypothesis, and analytical framework. This deductive

Table 1.1 A model of how advocacy groups can use political marketing to support the public diplomacy and nation branding efforts of the Israeli and the Palestinian governments

Components	Theories and concepts
Marketing orientation	Advocacy groups can attract new members by adopting either product, sales, or market-orientations which guide their behaviour and use of political marketing: • Product-oriented groups are motivated by their cause and allow their political values and beliefs to dictate their actions and policies. They are reluctant to change their communicational and relational activities to suit membership subscription, public or government opinion. OR • Sales-oriented groups stick to their cause and message but are more willing to use targeted communicational and relational activities to recruit supporters to their cause. OR • Market-oriented groups use market intelligence to identify their supporters' demands and needs. They also design their cause including the campaigning and membership package to recruit supporters. They also communicate campaign progress to retain the support of their members.
"Segmentation, targeting, and positioning"	(a) Segmenting the market into smaller sections which can be targeted in terms of product, message, and medium. Tailoring their product and message to meet the needs and expectations of different markets. (b) Targeting segments that are sympathetic towards their stated goals and interests by strategically allocating resources and products to reaching them. (c) Positioning: Targeting their product at segments most receptive to their cause. This can include either altering the product itself to cater for the market ("real positioning") or altering perceptions of the product ("psychological positioning")

(*continued*)

Table 1.1 (continued)

Components	Theories and concepts
Internal marketing	Using a range of ideological, material, or democratic incentives to encourage activists and members to carry out external communicational and relational activities: • Material incentives involve paying senior-ranking members including directors, researchers, and consultants. OR • A base strategy involves giving internal stakeholders what they want and designing the advocacy group's product to fit their needs and expectations. OR • An empty vessel strategy involves creating a vague product that allows people to project their own ideas, wants, and demands onto it. OR • Dignified democracy involves using solidarity incentives (which is the satisfaction derived from feeling part of an organisation through activism) to motivate members and supporters. OR • Effective democracy involves real democratic consultation and joint creation and ownership of the product by all internal stakeholders.
Public diplomacy and nation branding	Helping state actors and sub-national actors to manage their international image and to advance their perceived national interests and aspirations through a range of communicational and relational activities including: • Working with foreign officials including diplomats and policy-makers. • Producing, sponsoring, or distributing a range of literature and media. • Promoting a county or ethnic group's culture, heritage, and identity. • Undertaking image management in response to crises and conflicts. • Sponsoring speaking engagements, cultural and education fairs, expos, and political-oriented tourism to promote sympathy.

approach informed this research's comparative case studies methodology which utilised content analysis and elite interviews.

This research also takes a comparative case study approach, testing the researcher's analytical framework against four groups. To ensure balance, two pro-Israel and two pro-Palestinian groups from New Zealand and Australia were selected:

- Palestine Solidarity Network Aotearoa (PSNA; formerly known as the New Zealand Palestine Solidarity Network or NZPSN), the national umbrella organisation for Palestinian solidarity groups in New Zealand.
- Israel Institute of New Zealand (IINZ), a pro-Israel think tank based in Auckland.
- Australia/Israel and Jewish Affairs Council (AIJAC), a Jewish community organisation and lobby group.
- The Australia Palestine Advocacy Network (APAN); the peak organisation for Palestinian solidarity groups and activists in Australia.

Criteria for selection included their broad scope of activity, approachability/accessibility, and linkages to state actors through advocacy and public diplomacy. The PSNA and APAN are national umbrella organisations, making them the leading organisations for Palestinian activism in New Zealand and Australia. The IINZ was selected due to its broad scope of activities including communications output and lobbying key New Zealand stakeholders. Finally, AIJAC was selected since the literature review identified it as the most active Zionist advocacy organisation in Australia due to its broad scope of communications and relational activities particularly its interest in lobbying political, media, and civil society elites.

In terms of content analysis, this book drew upon the author's PhD research which had analysed 1898 webpages, social media posts, audio-visual material, and various printed material produced by the four groups between 2010 and 2018. This eight-year timeframe covered a range of events and developments relating to Israel-Palestine during the 2010s, the previous decade. These primary sources were collected from the groups' websites, social media accounts, and literature including newsletters and magazines. Table 1.2 provides a brief tally of the types of sources that the content analysis used for writing each of the four case studies:

During the data collection process, content was copied from the groups' websites and stored on Word documents and PDF files. This research also transcribed audio-visual recordings from podcasts, YouTube, and Vimeo videos. Occasionally, the researcher used Internet Wayback Machine to retrieve lost Internet webpages. For Facebook posts and Twitter tweets,

Table 1.2 Tally of primary sources

Groups	Webpages	Facebook	Twitter	Videos and podcasts	Paraphernalia and media articles	Total (groups)
PSNA	14	153	Nil	111	32	310
IINZ	167	135	135	Nil	Nil	437
AIJAC	223	162	172	11	105	673
APAN	248	Nil	138	31	61	478
Total (sources)	652	450	445	153	198	1898

screenshots of the posts were copied onto Paint and Paint3D files where they were cropped and saved. These sources were then analysed against the author's analytical framework using NVivo software. The author's analytical framework was also used to generate "thick descriptions" in the empirical chapters. For each case study, an NVivo project file, source checklist sheet, and list of references were created to facilitate the collection and cataloguing of sources. To minimise the problem of "link rot," the author saved copies of webpages, audio-visual content, and social media posts in various Microsoft Word, JPG, and PNG files within his personal laptop, university database, and an external hard drive. The groups' main websites, social media accounts, and other publications are listed in the appendix section.

Due to the large volume of primary sources encountered in the Australian case studies, critical case sampling was used to generate samples from AIJAC's website, Twitter, and Facebook accounts, and APAN's Twitter account. For both case studies, critical case sampling focused on stories and content relating to New Zealand, Australia, Israel, the Palestinians, media engagement, and anti-Semitism. While the first three case studies consulted the groups' Facebook pages, the research did not look at APAN's Facebook since changes to Facebook's privacy policies made it impossible to retrieve Facebook data using extraction software such as Netvizz, Facepager, and Scrapestorm.

These primary sources were supplemented by interviews with available practitioners from three of the four case studies: the PSNA's National Chair John Minto, the Israel Institute's Director David Cumin, and APAN's Executive Officer Jessica Morrison. Since the author was unable to interview any current or former AIJAC practitioners due to the organisation's policy of not granting interviews, the researcher consulted several external sources including the works of Reich (2004), Rutland (2004), Markus (2004), Levey and Mendes (2004), Loewenstein (2006), Han and Rane (2013), Lyons (2017) and Gawenda (2020). As with the web, print, and audio-visual sources, the interviews were analysed against the codes and categories of the analytical framework via NVivo software.

Structure and Contents

This book consists of four empirical chapters looking at the case studies followed by a conclusion chapter. The second chapter looks at the Palestine Solidarity Network Aotearoa, while the third chapter will look at the Israel Institute of New Zealand. The fourth chapter looks at the Australia/Israel and Jewish Affairs Council, while the fifth chapter will look at the Australia Palestine Advocacy Network. Each of these case study chapters will give a brief outline of the organisation's history and activities. Based upon the structure of the theoretical framework, each chapter will discuss the marketing orientation, STP approach, and internal marketing strategy of the advocacy groups. Each chapter will also analyse the group's involvement in public diplomacy, using theories and concepts derived from several public diplomacy, nation branding, and advocacy scholars.

The conclusion will discuss the overall findings of the empirical chapters against the analytical framework and how they addressed the key goals of this book. The conclusion will also explain how this book contributes to the literature on political marketing, advocacy, public diplomacy, and nation branding.

References

Ahuvia, A. (2012). The social marketing of peace: Grassroots movements, US foreign policy and the Israeli-Palestinian conflict. *Israel Affairs, 18*(1), 54–73. https://doi.org/10.1080/13537121.2012.634272

Astorino-Courtois, A. (1996). Transforming international agreements into National Realities: Marketing Arab-Israeli peace in Jordan. *The Journal of Politics, 58*(4), 1035–1054. http://www.jstor.org/stable/2960148

Astorino-Courtois, A. (2000). Can peace be marketed? A preliminary analysis of Israelis and Palestinians. *Conflict Management and Peace Science, 18*(1), 97–122.

Auerbach, Y., & Yehuda, T. (2010). The relationship between electoral systems and political marketing: Israel 1988–2003. *Israel Affairs, 16*(3), 335–364. https://doi.org/10.1080/13537121.2010.487724

Avraham, E. (2009). Marketing and managing nation branding during prolonged crisis: The case of Israel. *Place Branding and Public Diplomacy, 5*(3), 202–212. https://doi.org/10.1057/pb.2009.15

Awad, S. (2015). Public diplomacy and the question of Palestine. *International Humanities Studies, 2*(3), 21–40.

Badder, A. R. (2014). *Being Jewish in New Zealand*. [Unpublished master's thesis]. University of Auckland.

Balmas, M., & Sheafer, T. (2010). Candidate image in election campaigns: Attribute agenda setting, affective priming, and voting intentions. *International Journal of Public Opinion Research, 22*(2), 204–229. https://doi.org/10.1093/ijpor/edq009

Bannon, D. P. (2004, April 4–8). *Marketing segmentation and political marketing* [Paper presentation] (pp. 1–23). UK Political Studies Association conference, University of Lincoln.

Bard, M. (2010). *The Arab lobby: The invisible Alliance that undermines America's interests in the Middle East*. Broadside Books.

Barnes, P. (2014). *The changing face of Palestinian leadership: The boycott, divestment and sanctions movement*. [Unpublished master's thesis]. Massey University.

Bartle, J., & Griffiths, D. (2002). Social-psychological, economic and marketing models of voting behaviour compared. In N. J. O'Shaughnessy & S. C. M. Henneberg (Eds.), *The idea of political marketing* (pp. 19–37). Praeger.

Beirman, D. (2000). Destination marketing: The marketing of Israel in Australia and the south-west Pacific. *Journal of Vacation Marketing, 6*(2), 145–153. https://doi.org/10.1057/pb.2009.15

Beirman, D. (2002). Marketing of tourism destinations during a prolonged crisis: Israel and the Middle East. *Journal of Vacation Marketing, 8*(2), 167–176.

Ben-Moshe, D. (2004). Pro-Israelism as a factor in Australian Jewish political attitudes and behaviour. In G. B. Levey & P. Mendes (Eds.), *Jews and Australian politics* (pp. 127–142). Sussex Academic Press.

Brin, E. (2006). Politically-oriented tourism in Jerusalem. *Tourist Studies, 6*(3), 215–243. https://doi.org/10.1177/1468797607076672

Burla, S. (2015). Israeli government and diaspora mobilisation: The flotilla to Gaza and Australian Jewry as a case study. In S. Burla & D. Lawrence (Eds.), *Australia & Israel: A diasporic, cultural and political relationship* (pp. 50–70). Sussex Academic Press.

Campo, S., & Alvarez, M. D. (2014). Can tourism promotions influence a Country's negative image? An experimental study on Israel's image. *Current Issues in Tourism, 17*(3), 201–219. https://doi.org/10.1080/13683500.2013.766156

Cobb, R., & Elder, C. (1972). *Participation in American politics: The dynamics of agenda building*. John Hopkins University Press.

Creswell, J. W. (2009). *Research design: Qualitative, quantitative, and mixed methods approaches*. Sage Publications.

Cull, N. J. (2009). *Public diplomacy: Lessons from the past*. Figueroa Press.

Cummings, J. (2016). Israel's public diplomacy: The problems of Hasbara, 1966–1975. Rowan & Littlefield.

Dinnie, K. (2016). *Nation branding: Concepts, issues, and practice* (2nd ed.). Routledge.

Faitaua, D. (2015, September 29). Protest as Victoria University hosts Israeli soldiers. *One News*. https://www.tvnz.co.nz/one-news/new-zealand/protest-as-victoria-university-hosts-israeli-soldiers-q13072.

Gawenda, M. (2020). *The power broker: Mark Leibler, an Australian Jewish life*. Monash University Press.

Gilboa, E. (2001). Diplomacy in the media age: Three models of uses and effects. *Diplomacy and Statecraft, 12*(2), 1–28. https://doi.org/10.1080/0959229010840620

Gilboa, E. (2006). Public diplomacy: The missing component in Israel's foreign policy. *Israel Affairs, 12*(4), 717–719. https://doi.org/10.1080/13533310600890067

Gilboa, E. (2008). Searching for a theory of public diplomacy. *The Annals of the American Academy, 616*(1), 55–77. https://doi.org/10.1177/0002716207312142

Greene, A. (2016). *December 30*. Australia distances itself from Obama administration's stance against Israeli settlements. https://www.abc.net.au/news/2016-12-30/australia-rejects-obama-stance-against-israeli-settlements/8153504

Greenfield, S. & Rothman, J. (2012). *Israeli Hasbara: Myths and facts: A report on the Israeli Hasbara apparatus 2012* (Molad: the Center for the Renewal of Israeli Democracy working paper 1). http://www.molad.org/images/upload/researches/79983052033642.pdf.

Hadari, G., & Turgeman, A. (2016). Chaos is the message: The crisis of Israeli public diplomacy. *Israel Journal of Foreign Affairs, 10*(3), 393–404. https://doi.org/10.1080/23739770.2016.1263918

Hafsa, L. B. (2014). The role of Arab American Advocacy Groups in shaping American foreign policy. *Society, 51*(5), 513–523. https://doi.org/10.1007/s12115-014-9817-7

Hallward, M. C. (2013). *Transnational activism and the Israeli-Palestinian conflict*. Palgrave Macmillan.

Han, E., & Rane, H. (2013). *Making Australian foreign policy on Israel-Palestine: Media coverage, public opinion and interest groups. Islamic studies series*. (Book 13. Melbourne University Press.

Hitchcock, J. (2016). Social media rhetoric of the transnational Palestinian-led boycott, divestment, and sanctions movement. *Social Media + Society*, *2*(1), 1–12. https://doi.org/10.1177/2056305116634367

Hunt, T. (2015, September 28). Israeli troops at Vic Uni an 'apology for military violence' – academic. *The Dominion Post*. http://www.stuff.co.nz/dominion-post/news/72470948/israeli-troops-at-vic-uni-an-apology-for-military-violence%2D%2Dacademic

Keck, M. E., & Sikkink, K. (1998). *Activists beyond Borders: Advocacy networks in international politics*. Cornell University Press.

King, E. (2016). *The pro-Israel lobby in Europe: The politics of religion and Christian Zionism in the European Union*. I.B. Tauris.

Lang, G., & Lang, K. (1983). *The battle for public opinion: The president, the press and the polls during Watergate*. Columbia University Press.

Lawrence, D. (2015). Rewriting the rules of engagement: New Australian Jewish connections with Israel. In S. Burla & D. Lawrence (Eds.), *Australia & Israel: A diasporic, cultural and political relationship* (pp. 13–31). Sussex Academic Press.

Lees-Marshment, J. (2001). The marriage of politics and marketing. *Political Studies*, *49*, 692–713.

Lees-Marshment, J. (2003). Marketing good works: New trends in how interest groups recruit supporters. *Journal of Public Affairs*, *3*(4), 358–361.

Lees-Marshment, J. (2004). *The political marketing revolution: Transforming the government of the UK*. Manchester University Press.

Lees-Marshment, J. (2014). *Political marketing: Principles and applications* (2nd ed.). Routledge.

Lees-Marshment, J., Elder, E., Chant, L., Osborne, D., Savoie, J., & van der Linden, C. (2018). Political parties and their customers: The alignment of party policies with supporter, target and undecided market preferences. In J. Lees-Marshment (Ed.), *Political marketing and management in the 2017 New Zealand election* (pp. 23–41). Palgrave Macmillan.

Levey, G. B. (2004). Jews and Australian multiculturalism. In G. B. Levey & P. Mendes (Eds.), *Jews and Australian politics* (pp. 179–197). Sussex Academic Press.

Levey, G. B., & Mendes, P. (2004). The Hanan Ashrawi affair: Australian Jewish politics on display. In G. B. Levey & P. Mendes (Eds.), *Jews and Australian politics* (pp. 215–230). Sussex Academic Press.

Lincoln, S. Y., & Guba, E. G. (1985). *Naturalistic inquiry*. Sage.

Loewenstein, A. (2006). *My Israel Question*. Melbourne University Press.

Louvet, M.-V. (2016). *Civil society, post-colonialism and transnational solidarity: The Irish and the Middle East conflict*. Palgrave Macmillan. https://doi.org/10.1057/978-1-137-55109-2

Lyons, J. (2017). *Balcony over Jerusalem*. Harper Collins Publishers Australia.

Macintyre, R. (1986, May). *Australasia and the question of Palestine* (AMESA Working Papers No. 6), pp. 1–27.
Macintyre, R. (1987). *New Zealand and the Middle East: Politics, energy and trade.* Australasian Middle East Studies Association.
Markus, A. (2004). Anti-Semitism and Australian Jewry. In G. B. Levey & P. Mendes (Eds.), *Jews and Australian politics* (pp. 109–126). Sussex Academic Press.
Matthews, I., & Arvanitakis, J. (2015). Academic boycott, divestment and sanctions: Implications for Australian-Israeli relations. In I. S. Burla & D. Lawrence (Eds.), *Australia & Israel: A diasporic, cultural and political relationship* (pp. 211–225). Sussex Academic Press.
Mearsheimer, J. J., & Walt, S. M. (2007). *The Israel lobby and U.S. foreign policy.* Farrar, Straus & Giroux.
Mendes, P. (2006). A case study of ethnic stereotyping: The campaign for an academic boycott of Israel. *Australian Journal of Jewish Studies, 20*, 141–168. https://research.monash.edu/en/publications/a-case-study-of-ethnic-stereotyping-the-campaign-for-an-academic-
Mendes, P. (2016). An updated history of the Australian Jewish Democratic Society, 2000-16. *Australian Jewish Historical Society Journal, 23*(1), 111–148. https://research.monash.edu/files/16004432/AJDS_History_pdf
Mendes, P., & Dyrenfurth, N. (2015). *Boycotting Israel is wrong: The progressive path to peace between Palestinians and Israelis.* New South Publishing.
MFAT – Ministry of Foreign Affairs & Trade. (n.d.) *Middle East.* Retrieved May 23, 2016, from https://www.mfat.govt.nz/en/countries-and-regions/middle-east/.
Miller, R. (2004). *Ireland and the Palestine question, 1948–2004.* Irish Academic Press.
Mozes, T., & Weimann, G. (2010). The E-marketing strategy of Hamas. *Studies in Conflict & Terrorism, 33*(3), 211–225. 10.1080/10576100903555762.
Nimijean, R. (2005). Articulating the "Canadian way": CanadaTM and the political manipulation of the Canadian identity. *British Journal of Canadian Studies, 18*(1), 26–52.
Nimijean, R. (2006). The politics of branding Canada: The international - domestic nexus and the rethinking of Canada's place in the world. *Mexican Journal of Canadian Studies, 11*, 67–85.
Ollins, W. (2002). Branding the nation – The historical context. *Brand Management, 9*(4–5), 241–248.
Orkibi, E. (2015). New politics', new media – New political language? A rhetorical perspective on candidates' self-presentation in electronic campaigns in the 2013 Israeli elections. *Israel Affairs, 21*(2), 277–292. https://doi.org/10.1080/13537121.2015.1008242

Pamment, J. (2013). *New public diplomacy in the 21ˢᵗ century*. Routledge.
Paul, D. M., & Paul, R. A. (2009). *Ethnic lobbies & US foreign policy*. Lynne Rienner Publishers.
Pettitt, R. T. (2015). Internal part political relationship marketing: Encouraging activism amongst local party members. In J. Lees-Marshment (Ed.), *Routledge handbook of political marketing* (pp. 137–150). Routledge.
Radio New Zealand. (2017, June 14). *Israel agrees to restore diplomatic ties with NZ*. https://www.rnz.co.nz/news/political/332971/israel-agrees-to-restore-diplomatic-ties-with-nz.
Rainbow, S. (1997). *The changing attitude of New Zealand towards Israel from 1948–1993* (Occasional Paper No. 1).
Reich, C. (2002). *Australia and Israel: An ambiguous relationship*. Melbourne University Press.
Reich, C. (2004). Inside AIJAC – An Australian Jewish Lobby Group. In G. B. Levey & P. Mendes (Eds.), *Jews and Australian politics* (pp. 198–214). Sussex Academic Press.
Ritchie, C. D. (1986). *New Zealand and South West Asia: Defence, energy and trade. A perspective on the forces at work in determining New Zealand's foreign policy towards South West Asia between 1947 and 1956 with particular attention New Zealand's official policy of even-handedness in the Palestine conflict* [Unpublished master's thesis]. University of Auckland.
Rockower, P. S. (2012). Recipes for gastrodiplomacy. *Place Branding and Public Diplomacy, 8*(3), 235–246. https://doi.org/10.1057/pb.2012.17
Rubenstein, C., & Fleischer, T. (2007). A distant affinity: The history of Australia-Israeli relations. *Jewish Political Studies Review, 19*(3–4), 101. http://jcpa.org/article/a-distant-affinity-the-history-of-australian-israeli-relations-2/
Rutland, S. D. (2004). Who speaks for Australian Jewry. In G. B. Levey & P. Mendes (Eds.), *Jews and Australian politics* (pp. 29–43). Sussex Academic Press.
Sahhar, M. (2015). An Alliance of forgetting. In S. Burla & D. Lawrence (Eds.), *Australia & Israel: A diasporic, cultural and political relationship* (pp. 175–190). Sussex Academic Press.
Sarantakos, S. (2005). *Social research* (3rd ed.). Palgrave Macmillan.
Schleifer, R. (2014). Propaganda, PSYOP, and political marketing: The Hamas campaign as a case in point. *Journal of Political Marketing, 13*(1–2), 152–173. https://doi.org/10.1080/15377857.2014.866413
Schonker-Schreck, D. (2004). Political marketing and the media: Women in the 1996 Israeli elections – A case study. *Israel Affairs, 10*(3), 159–177. https://doi.org/10.1080/1353712042000242626
Schulman, S. (2012). *Israel/Palestine and the queer international*. Duke University Press.

Shai, N. (2018). *Hearts and minds: Israel and the battle for public opinion* (I. Moskowitz, Trans.). State University of New York Press. http://web.b.ebscohost.com.ezproxy.auckland.ac.nz/ehost/ebookviewer/ebook?sid=efe0c661-9117-4a43-9233-7bff16b16263%40pdc-v-sessmgr03&vid=0&format=EK.

Smits, K., & Jansen, A. (2012). Staging the nation at expos and world's fairs. *National Identities*, *14*(2), 173–188. https://doi.org/10.1080/14608944.2012.677817

Stuff. (2016, December 24). *Israeli ambassador to New Zealand recalled after UN security resolution*. https://www.stuff.co.nz/world/87931970/israeli-ambassador-to-new-zealand-recalled-after-un-security-resolution.

Szondi, G. (2008). *Public diplomacy and nation branding: Conceptual similarities and differences* (Discussion Papers in Diplomacy, Netherlands Institute of International Relations Cligendael). https://www.clingendael.nl/sites/default/files/20081022_pap_in_dip_nation_branding.pdf.

Toldeno, M., & McKie, D. (2009). The Israeli PR experience: Nation building and professional values. In K. Sriramesh & D. Verčič (Eds.), *The handbook of global public relations: Theory, research, and practice* (2nd ed., pp. 243–261). Routledge.

Toledano, M. (2005). Challenging accounts: Public relations and a tale of two revolutions. *Public Relations Review*, *31*, 463–470. https://doi.org/10.1016/j.pubrev.2005.08.004

Toledano, M. (2010). Military spokespeople and democracy: Perspectives from two Israeli wars. In R. L. Heath (Ed.), *The SAGE handbook of public relations* (2nd ed., pp. 585–598). SAGE Publications.

Toledano, M., & McKie, D. (2013). *Public relations and nation building: Influencing Israel*. Routledge.

Trotter, S. A. (2019). *Zionism 'at the uttermost ends of the earth': A New Zealand social history c.1900–1948*. [Unpublished PhD thesis]. University of Auckland.

van Ham, P. (2001). The rise of the brand state: The postmodern politics of image and reputation. *Foreign Affairs*, *80*(5), 2–6. http://www.jstor.org/stable/20050245

Van Voorthuysen, H. (2011). *Just a damned nuisance: New Zealand's changing relationship with Israel from July 1947 until May 2010*. [Unpublished master's thesis]. Victoria University of Wellington.

Voltolini, B. (2016). *Lobbying in EU foreign policy-making: The case of the Israeli-Palestinian conflict*. Routledge.

Zaharna, R. S. (2003). Palestinian public diplomacy: A tale of two intifadas, draft chapter, 2003, courtesy of the author, 1-18; later published as *Historia de dos intifadas: Un analisis mediatico del ascenso y la cainda de la imagen palestina* [A tale of two intifadas: A communication analysis of the rise and fall of the

Palestinian image]. In I. Alvarez-Ossorio (Ed.), *Informe Sobre El Conflicto de Palestina* (pp. 239–256). Eiciones del Oriente y del Meditarraneo.

Zaharna, R. S. (2009). Mapping out a Spectrum of public diplomacy initiatives: Information and relational communication frameworks. In N. Snow & P. M. Taylor (Eds.), *Routledge handbook of public diplomacy* (pp. 86–99). Routledge.

Zaharna, R. S., Hammad, A. I., & Masri, J. (2009). Palestinian public relations – Inside and out. In K. Sriramesh & D. Verčič (Eds.), *The handbook of global public relations: Theory, research, and practice* (Vol. 2, pp. 220–242). Routledge.

CHAPTER 2

Palestine Solidarity Network Aotearoa

Abstract This chapter analyses the political marketing, public diplomacy, and nation branding activities of the Palestine Solidarity Network Aotearoa (PSNA), the premier Palestinian solidarity network in New Zealand. This chapter draws upon a content analysis of webpages, paraphernalia, social media posts, and audio-visual content produced by the Network between 2010 and 2018. These primary sources were supplemented by an interview with the PSNA's national chair John Minto. This chapter will give a brief description of the PSNA before discussing the group's market-orientation, "segmentation, targeting, and position" (STP), internal marketing, public diplomacy, and nation branding strategies and activities.

Keywords Palestinian solidarity • BDS (Boycott, Divestment, and Sanctions) • Product-orientation • Segments • Psychological positioning • Base strategy

Overview

The Palestine Solidarity Network Aotearoa (PSNA) is a network of Palestinian solidarity organisations in New Zealand. It was founded as the New Zealand Palestine Solidarity Network (NZPSN) following the

© The Author(s), under exclusive license to Springer Nature Switzerland AG 2022
A. Lim, *Political Marketing and Public Diplomacy by Pro-Israel and Pro-Palestinian Advocacy Groups*, Palgrave Studies in Political Marketing and Management,
https://doi.org/10.1007/978-3-031-15332-7_2

Conference on Palestine in 2013 to facilitate cooperation among local Palestinian solidarity groups and promote support for a free Palestine in New Zealand. In June 2019, the Network formalised its national structure and revamped itself as the PSNA. The PSNA advocates recognising the Palestinian Right of Return, ending the Israeli military occupation, alleged discrimination, and human rights abuses against the Palestinians, and proposes a one-state solution to the Israel-Palestine conflict (NZPSN, n.d.-a; PSNA, 2019, June 27). The PSNA has consisted of several groups including Kia Ora Gaza, the Auckland-based Palestine Human Rights Campaign (PHRC), Palestine Human Rights Campaign Waikato, the Palestine Solidarity Network Christchurch, Wellington Palestine, Te Tau Ihu (Nelson) Palestine Solidarity, Palestine Solidarity Whangarei, Tauranga Moana 4 Palestine, Dunedin for Justice in Palestine, Global Peace & Justice (GP&J) Auckland, University of Auckland Students for Justice in Palestine (SJP), and Victoria University Students for Justice in Palestine (Wellington Palestine, n.d.; NZPSN, 2018, March; Ahed Tamimi Dunedin rally, personal communication, February 3, 2018). According to Minto (personal communication, February 28, 2020), the PSNA's member organisations are autonomous with each group making their own decisions and running themselves. They are bound together by a common cause: solidarity with the Palestinians and working to improve public support in New Zealand for the Palestinians.

Marketing Orientation

While the content analysis findings initially suggested that the PSNA pursued a sales-orientation, John Minto (personal communications, February 28, 2020) clarified that the Network pursued a product-orientation. A product-oriented organisation focuses on advancing its cause with little interest in changing their behaviour to suit membership subscriptions, public or government opinion (Lees-Marshment, 2004, 2014). During the interview, Minto clarified that the Network did not target a specific audience or demographic, stating that *"the people that we target are people who have already shown an interest. That is people who have turned up to a public meeting or who approach us at a protest and put their names down. So people who sort of identify as supporters and they choose to join our mailing list. So we don't go door to door and we don't go out to talk. We work with people who have already shown an interest."* Minto also explained that the Network was a voluntary organisation with the only paid employee being the Network's Secretary Neil Scott. The Network regarded door-to-door recruiting and cold calls as an ineffective way of doing things, with Minto describing their support base as "self-identified" Palestinian solidarity supporter. Though the PSNA uses its website, social media, and newsletters to disseminate its messages and promote its public gatherings, the focus is on communicating the Network's product of advancing Palestinians rights and self-determination through the transnational Boycott, Divestment and Sanctions (BDS) campaign, which is discussed in further detail below.

The interview and content analysis showed that the PSNA followed the four-stage process associated with product-oriented charities, as outlined in Table 2.1:

Analysis

In terms of marketing orientation, the PSNA followed the four stages of product-oriented advocacy groups. Firstly, it has a product in the form of advancing Palestinian rights and statehood through the BDS campaign. Second, it has used a wide range of communication and relational activities to raise awareness of its product to the public. Third, the Network has staged highly visible public events and lobbied civil society and governmental actors to advance its cause and goals. Finally, the PSNA engages in delivery by using its own communications to extol the successes of their campaigns. Lees-Marshment's product-oriented model is useful for classifying the PSNA as group.

Segmentation, Targeting, and Positioning (STP)

Based on the content analysis and the interview with the PSNA's National Chair John Minto, the Network has engaged all three stages of Bartle and Griffiths' (2002) "segmentation, targeting, and positioning" (STP) process.

Segmentation

According to Minto (personal communication, February 28, 2020), the PSNA sought to recruit individuals who were sympathetic to the Palestinian cause, attended its public meetings and protests, and registered for their email mailing list. Minto added that the Network also avoided door-to-door canvassing and cold calls, regarding them as ineffective and costly in

Table 2.1 The PSNA analysed using Lees-Marshment's product-oriented framework

Stages	Definitions	Examples
Product design	Design a wide range of behaviour in accordance to what they think is right, works best, and helps it to achieve its goals, as well as receive enough money to do it.	Advancing Palestinian rights and self-determination through the BDS campaign as part of a global Palestinian solidarity movement (NZPSN, n.d.-a).
Communication	Information is there if people want to get it.	Using its website (https://www.psna.nz/), Facebook account (https://www.facebook.com/NZPalestine/), email newsletters, media releases, paraphernalia, and public gatherings to communicate its message (Minto, personal communication, February 28, 2020).
Campaign	Inform and lobby individuals, groups, governments, and other actors about what they want. This may also include short-term campaigns.	Organising various public activities including public meetings, protests, speaking events, and tours to promote their cause and attract supporters (NZPSN, n.d.-f; NZPSN, 2017f; Palestinehumanrights, 2010a, 2011a). Lobbying various political and civil society actors on Palestinian issues including UN Security Council Resolution 2334 and the International Holocaust Remembrance Alliance's (IHRA's) definition of anti-Semitism (Minto, personal communication, February 28, 2020).
Delivery	Deliver what it thinks is best	Using its website, social media, and email newsletters to inform supporters and the public of their activities and successes.

terms of resources and manpower. As a network of autonomous groups that made their own organisational decisions, the Network welcomed groups which shared its cause and goals of promoting Palestinian rights and self-determination. While Minto's interview suggests that the PSNA avoided segmenting its target audience, a content analysis of the author's field notes from seven Network-sponsored public meetings and speaking engagements suggests that the PSNA has identified several "friendly" and "hostile" segments. These field notes observations are outlined in Table 2.2:

Table 2.2 Outline of field note observations from PSNA public meetings and speaking engagements

Events and functions	Speaker and audience demographics
Justice for Palestine talk, personal communication, April 3, 2016	Speakers included Kia Ora Gaza organiser Roger Fowler, Labour Member of Parliament (MP) Su'a William Sui, First Union secretary-general Robin Reed, Pax Christi national convenor Kevin McBride, Wellington Palestinian trade unionist Nadia Abu-Shanab, Green Party MP Marama Davidson, and Palestinian guest speaker Ali Abunimah. The audience was mainly pro-Palestinian with New Zealand Jewish Council (NZJC) member Juliet Moses being clapped down for arguing that the "Right of Return" would lead to Israel's destruction as a Jewish state.
Kia Ora Gaza fundraiser dinner, personal communication, August 28, 2016	Speakers included one of the Māori TV journalists who took part in the 2015 Gaza Flotilla and Green MP Davidson. South African youth Hamid read a poem about the life of a Palestinian girl while two Indian singers named Thingy S. and Longman played three songs. The event was organised by Fowler and members of the Muslim Umma youth group. University of Auckland law academic and anti-TPPA (Trans-Pacific Partnership Agreement) campaigner Jane Kelsey was also an audience member.
Rafeef Ziadah concert, personal communication, April 9, 2017	One of the guest speakers was Save Our Unique Landscapes (SOUL) spokesperson Brendan Corbin, who linked the Māori land struggle to the Palestinian one. The poet Mohammed Hassan gave a short poem in Arabic and English about travelling through airport terminals. The Palestinian-Canadian speaker Rafeef Ziadah also made references that resonated with left-wing audiences such as "who killed Allende, funded Osama, and lynched black people." There was also a performance at the end by the local Philistia Dekba Squad, which consists of Palestinian New Zealanders.
Al Aqsa Solidarity Rally, personal communication, July 29, 2017	This rally was attended by about 100–150 local New Zealand Palestine solidarity activists (including Pakeha/European New Zealanders and Māori) and members of the Arab and Muslim communities. Besides the then PSNA coordinator Debbie Abbas, other speakers included a former Christian Zionist named George, Avigail Allen from Dayenu (Jews against the Occupation) and a leader of the Muslim community. Attendees included PSNA member Leslie Bravery and his wife Marion. Several pro-Israel advocates including Julie Moses and Israel Institute of New Zealand (IINZ) Director David Cumin argued with the Palestinian solidarity advocates.

(*continued*)

Table 2.2 (continued)

Events and functions	Speaker and audience demographics
Ahed Tamimi Dunedin rally, personal communication, February 3, 2018	This rally was attended by about 30–40 people including members of the International Socialist Organisation (ISO) branch, Black Star Books, Green Party, and the Dunedin Muslim community. The local PSNA organiser was Simon Edmunds, a Chinese language lecturer.
Lorde Help Us talk, personal communication, March 21, 2018	Organisers were Debbie Abbas and University of Auckland dance Associate-Professor Nicholas Rowe. Speakers were Huwaida Arraf and Justine Sachs. The crowd was mainly pro-Palestinian but included several pro-Israel hecklers including Zionist Federation of New Zealand (ZFNZ) leader Rob Berg.
The Last Earth: A Palestinian story talk, personal communication, May 24, 2018	The Dunedin lecture was attended by about 50–55 people. It was hosted by Professor Richard Jackson of the University of Otago's National Centre for Peace and Conflict Studies (NCPCS). Most were middle-aged to elderly Pakeha but there were several young people including Palestinians, some Māori, an African, and one Chinese (the researcher who was only there to observe).

Based on these field notes, the most pro-Palestinian segments were left-wing political and civil society figures and groups (including the two left-wing political parties Labour and the Greens); members of the Arab and Muslim communities including the Palestinian diaspora; and dissident Jews such as Sachs and Allen who sympathised with the Palestinians and opposed Israel's policies and Zionism. The significant left-wing pro-Palestinian segments reflect the contemporary global left-wing sympathy for Palestinians, making the political left a natural ally for Palestinian advocates. Arab-Muslim sympathy for the Palestinian cause is motivated by both ethnic and religious solidarity with the Palestinian peoples. The presence of dissident Jews reflects the existence of the vocal minority of Jews around the world who disagree with the current trajectory of Israel's relationship with the Palestinians. By contrast, "hostile segments" consist of Zionist groups and advocates such as Jewish Council member Juliet Moses, IINZ Director David Cumin, and Zionist Federation leader Rob Berg.

These field notes were corroborated by a content analysis of the PSNA's webpages, paraphernalia, and audio-visual material. These showed that the Network had identified several civil society and political segments and figures whom it could collaborate or build coalitions with on issues relating to Palestine. Notable friendly civil society allies have included:

- **Palestinian solidarity groups**: Notable allies included the Wellington Palestine Group (WPG) and "Dayenu – NZ Jews Against the Occupation." The PSNA collaborated with the WPG during their 2016 New Zealand Super Fund campaign (NZPSN, n.d.-h, n.d.-i; WPG, 2016). The PSNA leaders Janfrie Wakim and Fowler attended a candlelight vigil organised by Dayenu to mark the 60th anniversary of the Six-Day War in June 2017 (NZPSN, 2017b). In return, Dayenu leader Justine Sachs spoke at the PSNA's Free Ahed Tamimi rally in February 2018 and the "Lorde Help Us" public meeting at the University of Auckland in March 2018 (NZPSN, 2018e; Palestinehumanrights, 2018c). Cooperation enables Palestinian solidarity groups to share resources while reinforcing the notion that they are working together to advance Palestinian rights and self-determination. The presence of dissident Jews such as Sachs helps to combat criticism that the Palestine solidarity movement is anti-Semitic.
- **Trade unions:** New Zealand Confederation of Trade Unions (NZCTU), Unite Union, and First Union. The First Union and NZCTU supported the PSNA's NZ Super Fund divestment efforts (Palestinehumanrights, 2014q). In addition, there was a large trade union presence at several PSNA-sponsored events during the 2010 Mavi Marmara Incident, the 2013 Veolia divestment protest, the 2014 Gaza War, and the 2018 Free Ahed Tamimi Auckland protest (Palestinehumanrights, 2010c, 2013, 2014c, 2014d, 2018b).
- **Faith groups:** Quaker Peace and Service, Pax Christi (NZPSN, 2018a, 2018b, 2018c).
- **Cause groups:** Wellington Peace Action, Auckland Peace Action, Women's International League for Peace and Freedom (WILPF), Working Together (NZPSN, 2018a, 2018b, 2018c, 2018d).

This collaboration reflects the BDS Movement's (n.d.) strategy of encouraging civil society institutions and companies such as local councils, churches, pension funds, banks, and universities to divest from all Israeli companies and international companies alleged to be involved in violating Palestinian rights. While these organisations do not focus on Palestinian issues, they may adopt the Palestinian cause as one among many contemporary issues such as climate change, poverty, war, and workers' rights. Thus, these civil society groups can be considered "friendly segments" who would support the PSNA's pro-Palestinian cause and activities.

Reflecting the PSNA's interest in influencing New Zealand political parties and policy-makers' positions towards Israel-Palestine, the PSNA also collaborated with several sympathetic Members of Parliament and candidates from left-wing New Zealand political parties:

- **New Zealand Labour Party**: Priyanca Radhakrishnan and David Shearer (Palestinehumanrights, 2014l, 2014n)
- **Green Party of Aotearoa New Zealand**: Keith Locke, Kennedy Graham, Catherine Delahunty, Davidson (Palestinehumanrights, 2010d, 2014b, 2014e, 2014i)
- **Mana Movement**: John Minto, Syd Keepa (Palestinehumanrights, 2014h, 2014k)
- **Socialist Aotearoa**: Joe Carolan (Palestinehumanrights, 2010c)

Several of these politicians spoke at PSNA-sponsored events, which were streamed on the PHRC's YouTube channel. Green MP Davidson also took part in Women's Flotilla to Gaza in 2016, which was sponsored by Kia Ora Gaza (Palestinehumanrights, 2016d). The presence of Labour and Green Party politicians at Network rallies and meetings shows that the network has cultivated relations with these two parliamentary parties. Labour is the major centre-left party in New Zealand politics while the Greens are a left-wing environmentalist party with a strong focus on social justice and human rights issues. In addition, the PSNA appears to have forged friendly relations with minor left-wing parties such as the Mana Movement and Socialist Aotearoa. There also appears to be an overlapping membership between trade unions and radical left parties, reflecting the historical connection between the trade union movement and left-wing politics. For example, National Chair Minto was also a member of the GP&J Auckland, Unite Union, and Deputy Leader of the Mana Movement (Palestinehumanrights, 2010f, 2014k). Similarly, Carolan was a member of both the Unite Union and Socialist Aotearoa (Palestinehumanrights, 2010c, 2012d). The presence of both centre-left and radical left politicians at Network events and rallies suggests that Palestinian solidarity is becoming a left-wing phenomenon, making left-wing parties and figures key pro-Palestinian segments.

Targeting

Second, the PSNA targeted these pro-Palestinian segments by producing pro-Palestinian informational output and organising a range of relational activities (including public meetings, protests, and lobbying campaigns) to reach them. On a communication front, the Network operated a website (https://www.psna.nz/), Facebook page (https://www.facebook.com/NZPalestine/), and an email mailing list. The PSNA website contains information about the Network's aims (including endorsement of the BDS movement), public activities, member groups, paraphernalia, and audio-visual material (NZPSN, n.d.-a, n.d.-b, n.d.-e). In addition, the PSNA disseminates leaflets and posters and encouraged its members and supporters to write letters to newspapers and call talkback radio on issues relating to Israel-Palestine. One of the PSNA's affiliates, the Auckland-based PHRC, also used its YouTube channel "Palestinehumanrights" (https://www.youtube.com/user/palestinehumanrights/videos) to promote the Network's protest and public speaking activities.

In terms of relational activities, the PSNA has used public demonstrations, speaking engagements, and film screenings to target sympathetic segments (John Minto, personal communications, February 28, 2020). The PSNA stages monthly rallies on the first Saturday of each month in Auckland's Aotea Square (NZPSN, 2018b). In addition, the PSNA and its allies have also organised other protest campaigns against Shahar Pe'er's participation in the 2010 ASB Tennis Tournament (NZPSN, n.d.-f), the sale of Israeli "Dead Sea products" and SodaStream soft drinks in New Zealand (NZPSN, n.d.-f; Palestinehumanrights, 2011a, 2011b), the Batsheva Dance Tour's 2014 Wellington tour (Palestinehumanrights, 2014a), and protests in response to international developments such as the 2010 Gaza flotilla raid, Israel's "Operation Pillar of Defense" in Gaza in November 2012, the 2014 Israel-Gaza conflict, the 2017 Temple Mount crisis, and the 2018 imprisonment of Palestinian teenager Ahed Tamimi (Palestinehumanrights, 2010e, 2012e, 2014m, 2014p, 2018d; Al Aqsa Solidarity Rally, personal communication, July 29, 2017; NZPSN, 2018b). These protests seek to raise awareness of the Palestinian cause by occupying public spaces (such as Auckland's Aotea Square, St Luke's and Sylvia Park shopping malls, and the University of Auckland). To publicise these protests, the PSNA uploaded images and video footage of them onto its Facebook page and the PHRC's YouTube channel. Several "friendly segments" including the Unite Union, First Union, Dayenu, and the Green

Party participated in these protests (Palestinehumanrights, 2014e, 2014g, 2014o, 2018c). These protest activities were often timed to coincide with widely publicised international events such as the 2014 Gaza conflict and the 2015 BDS worldwide campaign against the French multinational transport company Veolia International's bus operations in the Occupied Territories (NZPSN, n.d.-f; Palestinehumanrights, 2013). In short, the PSNA used its communications output and relational activities to target those who were sympathetic to Palestinian rights and self-determination.

As part of its relational activities, the PSNA works with sympathetic individuals and groups to advance the global Boycott, Divestment, and Sanctions (BDS) campaign in New Zealand. The BDS campaign is a global civil society initiative which seeks to advance Palestinian rights and self-determination by applying economic, social, and political pressure on Israel. The PSNA looks up to the BDS National Committee in Ramallah for guidance and leadership (NZPSN, n.d.-a, n.d.-c). The PSNA has supported the BDS campaign by:

- Staging protests in Auckland calling upon the French multinational transport company Veolia International to divest from bus operations in the Occupied Territories in 2015 (NZPSN, n.d.-c; Palestinehumanrights, 2013).
- Supporting international BDS efforts to convince the Danish-British security company G4S, Irish company CRH, and the French telecommunications company Orange to divest from Israel (NZPSN, n.d.-c).
- Opposing the proposed Film Cooperation agreement between New Zealand and Israel in solidarity with the BDS Call (NZPSN, n.d.-d, n.d.-e, n.d.-g).
- Called on Wellington stores to remove SodaStream products (NZPSN, n.d.-f).
- Opposing the planned "Innovation expedition" to Israel (NZPSN, 2016b, 2016c).
- Promoting the "BDS – Driving Global Justice for Palestine" held at the University of Sydney in late July 2017. The BDS Sydney conference was sponsored by the University of Sydney's Department of Peace and Conflict Studies, Sydney University Staff for BDS, and the Australia Palestine Advocacy Network (APAN). PSNA leader Wakim spoke at the conference (BDS Sydney, n.d.-a, n.d.-b; NZPSN, 2017c).

- Lobbying the New Zealand Super Fund to divest from banks and companies alleged to be complicit in supporting the Israeli occupation of the Palestinian Territories (NZPSN, n.d.-i). In 2012, they succeeded in convincing the NZ Super Fund to divest from three Israeli companies: Africa Israel Investments (and its subsidiary Danya Ce bus), El bit Systems Ltd., and Shikun & Binui (NZPSN, n.d.-h).

These activities show that the PSNA supports the goals and agenda of the BDS Movement and that it also regards the BDS National Committee as the voice of Palestinian civil society and by extension, ordinary Palestinians.

Positioning

In terms of positioning, the PSNA appears to practise "psychological positioning" which focuses on altering perceptions of their product (Bartle & Griffiths, 2002). As discussed, the PSNA's stated cause is to advance Palestinian rights and self-determination through the transnational BDS campaign. The PSNA also supports the Palestinian Right of Return, ending the Israeli military occupation, alleged discrimination, and human rights abuses against the Palestinians, and advocates a one-state solution to the Israel-Palestine conflict (NZPSN, n.d.-a; PSNA, 2019, June 27). The content analysis also found that several PSNA activists including Minto, Carolan, Wakim, Billy Hania, and Fowler have made emotionally charged statements likening Israel to Nazi Germany and Apartheid South Africa; identifying the Palestinian solidarity movement with popular causes such as the American and Irish civil rights, the anti-Apartheid, the nuclear-free, and the Māori rights movements, Zionism being a racist ideology built on ethnocentrism and genocide; and claiming that the "indigenous" Palestinians are being oppressed by Israeli "settler colonialism" (Palestinehumanrights, 2010b, 2012d, 2014n, 2014f, 2014j). These binary messages and narratives strike an emotional chord with sympathetic members of the public. Presenting the Palestinian cause as a struggle for human rights and self-determination appeals to those who regard advancing human rights and ending colonialism as key political imperatives. Likening Israel's treatment of the Palestinians to Nazi Germany and Apartheid South Africa also appeals to those who regard fighting racism and discrimination as key moral imperatives. Tying the Palestinian cause to past civil rights causes and movements such as the American civil rights, anti-Apartheid and Māori rights movements also helps establish the Palestinian cause as the latest in the global struggle for human rights and equality. In short, psychological positioning is used to promote sympathy for the PSNA's cause and advocacy work.

Analysis

The PSNA followed all three stages of the segmentation, targeting, and positioning process. Despite its limited resources and manpower, the Network conducted some rudimentary segmentation by collaborating with "friendly" segments such as other Palestinian solidarity groups, left-wing civil society and political groups and individuals, and dissident Jews. The Network also avoided "hostile" segments such as Zionist advocates and groups. The Network targeted friendly pro-Palestinian segments by allocating resources and products such as its website, email newsletters, Facebook posts, public gatherings, protest campaigns, and supporting the global BDS campaign. Finally, the PSNA conducted psychological positioning by linking the Palestinian cause to past civil rights causes and movements while using emotive language likening Israel to racist, authoritarian regimes.

INTERNAL MARKETING

In terms of internal marketing, the PSNA pursues a base strategy, which involves the leadership using a product that resonates with their core supporters to incentivise them. As with most political parties, participation in advocacy groups is motivated by solidarity and commitment towards the group's aims and goals (Pettitt, 2015, pp. 143–144). A base strategy also aligns with the Network's product-orientation which involves attracting members and supporters who support their goal of promoting Palestinian rights and self-determination through BDS.

Evidence for a base strategy is supported by a content analysis of the PSNA's "What is BDS?" page (NZPSN, n.d.-a) and three newsletters (NZPSN, 2018a, 2018b, 2018c). These showed that membership of the Network is based on members and supporters participating in a range of advocacy activities to advance Palestinian rights and self-determination including:

- Joining in pickets, demonstrations, meetings, and other actions when called
- Supporting the BDS Movement's boycott and divestment campaigns against Israel
- Telling local MPs their opinions on divestment and sanctions against Israel
- Setting up SJP chapters on campuses
- Writing letters to newspapers and calling talkback radio
- Keeping updated on their Facebook pages and websites
- Offering to help with leafleting and posters
- Donating towards their campaigns

Besides enabling activists and supporters to contribute to advancing the Network's cause and advocacy work on a local level, these activities also help to build a sense of community through solidarity and commitment to a shared cause. People and groups are drawn to the PSNA by its stated commitment to advancing the Palestinian cause and BDS Call at a local level.

The content analysis findings were corroborated by Minto (personal communication, February 28, 2020), who stated that "people are motivated by information" about the plight of the Palestinians. Besides educating the public about the situation in Palestine, the Network also sought to convince them that their advocacy work could help make a difference. Besides their Facebook page and email newsletter, Minto regarded the Network's guest speaking engagements as an important aspect of the organisation's work. He claimed that the PSNA promoted loyalty and purpose among its members and supporters by "being clear and focused in their communications with members and the general public." He also regarded maintaining a high public profile as essential to maintaining a sense of purpose and morale among their members. Minto's remarks confirm that the Network pursues a base strategy since it appeals to internal stakeholders' sympathy for Palestinian rights and self-determination. The PSNA has designed the group's product (producing communications and organising public events to promote the Palestinian cause through BDS) to appeal to their support for the Palestinian cause.

Analysis

In terms of internal marketing, the PSNA used ideological incentives to encourage activists and members to carry out external communications and relational activities. Pettitt's "base strategy" category of his internal marketing model proved useful for explaining the internal marketing activities of the PSNA. As a cause-oriented advocacy group, the Network's members and supporters were bound together by a shared adherence to the product of advancing Palestinian rights and self-determination via the BDS movement.

Public Diplomacy and Nation Branding

While the PSNA did not appear to have formal links or interactions with the Palestinian Authority and its General Delegation in Canberra, it has still conducted informal pro-Palestinian public diplomacy and nation branding by promoting Palestinian literature, media, culture, and heritage and sponsoring speaking engagements, cultural activities, and solidarity trips to the Palestinian Territories. The PSNA has used these communicational and relational activities to promote awareness and sympathy for the Palestinians within New Zealand while also strengthening ties with Palestinian civil society and other like-minded solidarity activists. Despite its lack of formal links with the Palestinian Authority, the PSNA looked up to the BDS National Committee for leadership and guidance, modelling many of its campaigns on BDS goals and criteria.

On the communicational front, the PSNA has promoted Palestinian literature and media by selling Palestinian products and sharing pro-Palestinian media stories through its website and Facebook platform. Besides fundraising, the PSNA website's "Shop page" (http://www.palestinesolidaritynz.net/shop.html) also helped to promote a favourable view of the Palestinian cause. As of June 2018, their page has been used to sell Palestinian literature such Ali Abunimah's *The Battle for Justice in Palestine* (2014) and Iyad Burnat's *Bil'in and the Nonviolent Resistance* (2016) and DVDs of Emad Burnat's film *5 Broken Cameras* (2011). Proceeds from the books and DVDs go back to the authors and can be deposited into the PSNA's bank account. This shows that the PSNA financially supports Palestinian authors and film-makers, which can be considered fundraising and coalition building as well. Previously, the "Shop page" had also sold copies of "Resistance"-themed Palestinian calendars on behalf of the Ramallah-based "Young Artists Forum," which runs evening art classes for Palestinian children. These calendars depicted pictures of Palestinian people including Mahmoud Darwish, buildings including the iconic Dome of Rock Mosque, fields, and tapestries (NZPSN, n.d.-b). These "Resistance" calendars were also advertised on their Facebook page at the end of the year when people are searching for calendars (NZPSN, 2017g). Besides revenue generation, Palestinian books, media, and calendars help to promote a favourable image of the Palestinians as an "indigenous" people resisting Israeli "oppression" and fighting for self-determination; a message that would resonate with Palestinian solidarity advocates. In addition to selling Palestinian literature and media, the PSNA has shared articles, social media posts, and audio-visual media promoting Palestinian rights and self-determination on their Facebook page including the following:

- Peter de Graaf's article on Māori carver, weaver, and artist Paitangi Ostick's documentary web-series *Pai in Palestine* exploring the art and lives of Palestinians living in the West Bank against the backdrop of the Israeli military occupation and settler expansion (Paitangi, n.d.; NZPSN, 2017f).
- PSNA activists Lois and Martin Griffith's radio interview with journalist and activist Julie Webb-Pullman, focusing on her efforts to pursue Israeli officials for alleged war crimes during the 2014 Gaza War (Griffith & Griffith, 2018; NZPSN, 2018j).
- Encouraging supporters to buy copies of the Palestinian activist Ramzy Baroud's book *The Last Earth* (NZPSN, 2018k).

These products and media content show that the PSNA's public diplomacy and nation branding focuses on humanising Palestinians as human beings, combating the dual media image of Palestinians as terrorists and "perpetual victims," and promoting the narrative of Palestinian resistance against Zionism. In addition, they also help promote Palestinian culture, heritage, and identity including territorial claims. While Ostick, Web-Pullman, and Griffiths provide examples of New Zealanders speaking up for the Palestinians, Baroud can be regarded as an example of a Palestinian voice to whom the PSNA helps provide a platform for. Thus, image management can also help reinforce the idea that New Zealanders and Palestinians are working together as allies in the global struggle for Palestinian rights and self-determination.

On the relational front, the Network has sponsored numerous speaking engagements, cultural, and public functions to promote awareness of the Palestinian cause and forge relations with overseas-based activists and groups including the following:

- Sponsoring guest speaking tours by Palestinian diaspora activists and civil society leaders including Ali Abunimah, Rafeef Ziadah, Huwaida Arraf, and Ramzy Baroud (NZPSN, 2016a, 2017a, 2018f, 2018g).
- Hosting Israeli dissident journalist and author Gideon Levy's public lecture at the Mount Eden War Memorial Hall on December 3, 2017, in conjunction with Quaker Peace and Action Service (NZPSN, 2017h; Palestinehumanrights, 2018a).
- Promoting Palestinian culture and media by publicising film-screening events like Waiheke's "Palestine Film Festival at Tivoli Theatre" in July 2017 and the screening of Paitangi Ostick's web documentary series *Pai in Palestine* in Whangarei in August 2017 (NZPSN, 2017d, 2017e).
- Sharing a post by Students for Justice Victoria University of Wellington (SJPVUW, 2017) advertising a family-friendly Palestinian-themed picnic on December 16, 2017, promoting Palestinian cuisine.

Besides fostering friendly relations with other Palestinian solidarity activists and groups, these talks and functions promote Palestinian cultural heritage and identity and combat negative imagery of the Palestinians resulting from media coverage and alleged Zionist "disinformation." These talks and functions also seek to promote the image of Palestinians as a resilient, cultured people resisting Israeli "settler-colonialism." The presence of Palestinian speakers and activists at these events helps give an authentic Palestinian voice. In addition, these events promote the PSNA's advocacy work in a positive light.

In addition, one of the Network's member organisations, Kia Ora Gaza, has organised several "politically oriented" trips and expeditions to the Palestinian Territories:

- Kia Ora Gaza (Palestinehumanrights, 2012a, 2012b, 2012c, 2018) participated in the 2010 Viva Palestina aid convoy to Gaza and organised a fact-finding mission to Gaza in November 2012.

- Sponsoring Green MP Davidson as the New Zealand representative on the "Women's Boat to Gaza" in October 2016 as part of a transnational campaign to oppose the Israeli naval blockade of Gaza (Palestinehumanrights, 2016a, 2016b, 2016c).
- Facilitating New Zealand participation in the "2018 Freedom Flotilla to Gaza" to challenge the Israeli blockade (NZPSN, 2018h, 2018i).

Kia Ora Gaza and the PSNA's participation in these politically oriented trips and expeditions constitute New Zealand's contribution to advancing the Palestinian cause globally. Besides building relationships with Palestinians and other solidarity advocates, these trips sought to "educate" New Zealand participants about the "facts on the ground."

Analysis

The PSNA engaged in informal public diplomacy and nation branding on both communicational and relational levels. While the Network did not appear to have formal links or interactions with the Palestinian Authority, they still promoted Palestinian interests and aspirations through their communications output and relational activities. The PSNA met the four criteria of public diplomacy. First, the Network produced, sponsored, and distributed a range of pro-Palestinian literature and media by selling Palestinian books and paraphernalia on their website and promoting pro-Palestinian social media content on their Facebook page. Second, it promoted Palestinian culture, heritage and identity including the Palestinian struggle for self-determination and territorial claims.

Third, the Network sponsored various public gatherings including speaking engagements, cultural functions, film screenings, and politically oriented tourism to the Palestinian Territories to raise awareness and promote sympathy for the Palestinians. While the PSNA conducted politically oriented tourism via fact-finding missions and solidarity trips to the Palestinian Territories, these were primarily intended as solidarity trips meant to strengthen ties between solidarity activists and the Palestinians themselves. Fourth, image management was embedded into these communicational and relational activities and focused on presenting the Palestinians as creative, resilient people resisting Israeli "Apartheid."

Conclusion

This chapter analysed the communications and advocacy activities of the Palestine Solidarity Network Aotearoa against the researcher's political marketing and public diplomacy framework. The PSNA met most of the criteria of this framework. First, in terms of marketing orientation, the Network met the characteristics of a product-oriented advocacy group. As a product-oriented group, the PSNA placed the Palestinian cause at the centre of its cause and advocacy work and showed little interest in moderating its product to win over the elites and public. An in-depth analysis of the PSNA's communications and relational activities showed that the group carried out all four stages of product-oriented political marketing by using their communications and relational activities to attract those who supported advancing Palestinian rights and self-determination through the BDS campaign.

Second, in terms of the "segmentation, targeting, and positioning" (STP) process, this research found that the Network conducted rudimentary segmentation by collaborating and networking with sympathetic civil society and political elements including the Arab-Muslim community, left-wing parties, NGOs and activists, and dissident Jews. The PSNA used its communications output and activities including the BDS campaign to target these sympathetic segments for mobilisation. Finally, the PSNA used psychological positioning to link the Palestinian cause to popular civil rights causes such as the anti-Apartheid movement while using emotive language likening Israel to authoritarian regimes such as Nazi Germany and Apartheid South Africa.

Third, the PSNA met the criteria of internal marketing by using ideological incentives to encourage activists and members to carry out external communications and relational activities. Pettitt's base strategy was the most relevant internal market model since it supported the research findings that the Network pursued a base strategy by appealing to what internal stakeholders wanted and designing the group's product to fit their needs and expectations. As part of its base strategy, the PSNA used its pro-Palestinian communications and advocacy work to appeal to their supporters' ideological commitment to Palestinian rights and self-determination. As a theory, a base strategy is useful for explaining how a cause-oriented group uses ideological commitment as the glue that binds together its support base.

Fourth, the PSNA practised informal public diplomacy and nation branding despite its lack of formal ties to the Palestinian Authority. The Network distributed pro-Palestinian literature and media; promoted Palestinian culture, heritage, and identity; and sponsored public gatherings including speaking engagements, cultural events, and politically oriented tourism. While it also conducted image management in response to crises and conflicts, this work was embedded into the above communications and relational activities. The PSNA supported Palestinian goals and interests by portraying the Palestinian people as a resilient, cultured people fighting for human rights, self-determination, and basic needs. By contrast, Israel was portrayed as a rogue, racist state that was perpetrating genocide and colonialism against the indigenous Palestinians.

References

Bartle, J., & Griffiths, D. (2002). Social-psychological, economic and marketing models of voting behaviour compared. In N. J. O'Shaughnessy & S. C. M. Henneberg (Eds.), *The idea of political marketing* (pp. 19–37). Praeger.

BDS Movement. (n.d.). *What is BDS?*. Retrieved May 12, 2018, from https://bdsmovement.net/what-is-bds

BDS Sydney. (n.d.-a). *BDS – Driving Global Justice for Palestine, 28–29 July 2017 website*. Retrieved June 15, 2018, from https://www.bdssydney.org/.

BDS Sydney. (n.d.-b). *Conference programme final for web*. Retrieved May 7, 2018, from https://www.bdssydney.org/wp-content/uploads/2017/07/Conference-programme-final-for-web.pdf

Griffith, L., & Griffith, M. (2018, May 21). *Earthwise-21-05-2018 Julie Webb Pullman* [Audio podcast]. Earthwise Plains FM 96.9. http://www.accessradio.org/Player.aspx?eid=505da3a4-1420-4f89-90f1-c3cf7a4b29d7

Kia Ora Gaza. (2018, June 15). *Kia Ora Gaza Projects*. https://kiaoragaza.wordpress.com/

Lees-Marshment, J. (2004). *The political marketing revolution: Transforming the government of the UK*. Manchester University Press.

Lees-Marshment, J. (2014). *Political marketing: Principles and applications* (2nd ed.). Routledge.

NZPSN. (n.d.-a). *What is BDS?*. Retrieved May 12, 2018, from http://www.palestinesolidaritynz.net/about.html

NZPSN. (n.d.-b). *Shop*. Retrieved March 27, 2018, from http://www.palestinesolidaritynz.net/shop.html

NZPSN. (n.d.-c). *BDS leaflet inside* [Brochure]. http://www.palestinesolidaritynz.net/img/res_pdf/BDS%20leaflet%20inside.pdf

NZPSN. (n.d.-d). *BFA leaflet front* [Brochure]. http://www.palestinesolidaritynz.net/img/res_pdf/Film%20Agreement%20Boycott%20campaign%20statement.pdf

NZPSN. (n.d.-e). *BFA leaflet back* [Brochure]. http://www.palestinesolidaritynz.net/img/res_pdf/BFA%20leaflet%20back.pdf

NZPSN. (n.d.-f). *Boycott Sodastream Flyer* [Brochure]. http://www.palestinesolidaritynz.net/img/res_pdf/Boycott%20Sodastream%20Flyer.pdf

NZPSN. (n.d.-g). *Film Agreement Boycott campaign statement* [Brochure]. http://www.palestinesolidaritynz.net/img/res_pdf/Film%20Agreement%20Boycott%20campaign%20statement.pdf

NZPSN. (n.d.-h). *Superfund leaflet front* [Brochure]. http://www.palestinesolidaritynz.net/img/res_pdf/Superfund%20leaflet%20front.pdf

NZPSN. (n.d.-i). *Superfund leaflet back.* [Brochure]. http://www.palestinesolidaritynz.net/img/res_pdf/Superfund%20leaflet%20back.pdf

NZPSN. (2016a). *US-Palestinian authors to address NZ audiences in April* [Press release]. http://www.palestinesolidaritynz.net/img/res_pdf/Press%20Release%20Ali%20Ramzy.pdf

NZPSN. (2016b, May 28). *Innovation expedition to Israel politically naïve* [Press release]. http://www.palestinesolidaritynz.net/img/res_pdf/Press%20release%20-%20Innovation%20expedition.pdf

NZPSN. (2016c, June 1). *Letter re innovation mission to Israel* [Press release]. http://www.palestinesolidaritynz.net/img/res_pdf/letter%20re%20innovation%20mission%20to%20Israel.pdf

NZPSN. (2017a, April 8). *April 8: An evening with Rafeef Ziadah Wellington.* https://www.facebook.com/NZPalestine/

NZPSN. (2017b, June 12). *Auckland candlelight vigil tonight – change of venue.* https://www.facebook.com/475410612595811/posts/1024576351012565/

NZPSN. (2017c, June 14). *BDS Conference in Sydney 28–29 July.* https://www.facebook.com/475410612595811/posts/1025891227547744/

NZPSN. (2017d, June 30). *Waiheke's Palestine Film Festival: final event tomorrow.* https://www.facebook.com/475410612595811/posts/1036762813127252/

NZPSN. (2017e, August 13). *To all those in or near Whangarei this is a must see! NZ Māori travel to Palestine and make an emotional connection with the Palestinian struggle!.* https://www.facebook.com/475410612595811/posts/1067623146707885/

NZPSN. (2017f, October 16). *Northland artist's Palestine series to screen at major film fest.* https://www.facebook.com/NZPalestine/posts/1100016793468520.

NZPSN. (2017g, November 23). *Resistance Art Calendars - $15.* https://www.facebook.com/NZPalestine/posts/1120851721385027

NZPSN. (2017h, December 3). *Over 300 people turned up to hear a moving talk by Gideon Levy this afternoon.* https://www.facebook.com/NZPalestine/posts/1126847990785400

NZPSN. (2018a, March). *NZPSN News March 2018* [Brochure].

NZPSN. (2018b, April). *NZPSN News April 2018* [Brochure].

NZPSN. (2018c, May). *NZPSN News May 2018* [Brochure].

NZPSN. (2018d, February 3). *Awesome #FreePalestine.* https://www.facebook.com/NZPalestine/posts/1163634140440118

NZPSN. (2018e, February 5). *Day of Action for Free Palestine in five NZ cities.* https://www.facebook.com/NZPalestine/posts/1164853606984838

NZPSN. (2018f, March 15). *March 21: Huwaida Arraf and Justine Sachs.* https://www.facebook.com/events/174734276489286/permalink/176898806272833

NZPSN. (2018g, April 26). *Ramzy Baroud NZ Tour.* https://www.facebook.com/events/606501949694121/

NZPSN. (2018h, May 21). *National Director of Unite Union in New Zealand, Mike Treen, is going on the next Flotilla to try and break the Seige [sic] of Gaza. Here, in conversation with leading Palestinian writer Ramzy Baroud, he details why the union movement of New Zealand should stand against Israeli Apartheid* [Video attached]. https://www.facebook.com/NZPalestine/posts/1229226503880881

NZPSN. (2018i, May 21). *Flotilla boats begin long voyage to Gaza.* https://www.facebook.com/475410612595811/posts/1228936893909842/

NZPSN. (2018j, May 23). *Excellent interview with Julie Webb-Pullman - The only New Zealand journalist in Gaza!.* https://www.facebook.com/NZPalestine/posts/1230089703794561

NZPSN. (2018k, May 25). *All of Ramzy Baroud's books sold out during his NZ tour this week. If you missed out, you can order yours at UBIQ Auckland University Bookshop or on line…* https://www.facebook.com/NZPalestine/posts/1231553263648205

Paitangi. (n.d.) Series One – Paitangi in Palestine [Video]. *He Ao Kotahi: The One World Project.* https://www.heaokotahi.co.nz/view-series/

Palestinehumanrights. (2010a, January 6). *Shahar Peer ASB Tour 2010 Auckland NZ Protest part 2.* YouTube. https://www.youtube.com/watch?v=te2PsaS3Rjk

Palestinehumanrights. (2010b, February 7). *Janfrie Wakim of Palestine Human Rights Campaign speaking on Waitangi Day 7 Feb 2010 Auckland New Zealand.* YouTube. https://www.youtube.com/watch?v=ZxJFpEaE37M

Palestinehumanrights. (2010c, June 4). *1–2 Speaking Out Against Israeli Flotilla Masscare Jun 2010.* YouTube. https://www.youtube.com/watch?v=z4V3EBBs4qk

Palestinehumanrights. (2010d, June 5). *1–5 Flotilla Protest Speech Keith Locke 5 Jun 2010.* YouTube. https://www.youtube.com/watch?v=tSSam_kxOqM

Palestinehumanrights. (2010e, June 5). *1–2 Flotilla Protest in Auckland -WHY MARCH-5 Jun 2010*. YouTube. https://www.youtube.com/watch?v=JKUXr_Ds6Tc

Palestinehumanrights. (2010f, June 5). *2–2 Flotilla Protest March to US Embassy 5 Jun 2010*. YouTube. https://www.youtube.com/watch?v=VcymFlivAKA

Palestinehumanrights. (2011a, April 28). *BDS Action - Auckland New, Zealand 23 April 2011*. YouTube. https://www.youtube.com/watch?v=N6k7DaW4xmA

Palestinehumanrights. (2011b, July 9). *BDS Action - Sylvia Park, Auckland New Zealand 9 July 2011*. YouTube. https://www.youtube.com/watch?v=AZMQHaorWWg

Palestinehumanrights. (2012a, June 7). *Kia Ora Gaza Team Aid convoy to Gaza from Auckland NZ 8 Jun*. YouTube. https://www.youtube.com/watch?v=wSwSz1Aokmw

Palestinehumanrights. (2012b, June 12). *Kia Ora Gaza convoy 2012 - Auckland Airport Welcomeback [sic] reception*. YouTube. https://www.youtube.com/watch?v=4M97PoS305k.

Palestinehumanrights. (2012c, June 30). *Kia Ora Gaza Reception Auckland 20 Jun 2012*. YouTube. https://www.youtube.com/watch?v=zNw_st042sE

Palestinehumanrights. (2012d, November 24). *Auckland protest in solidarity with Gaza Speaker Joe Carolan 24 Nov 2012*. YouTube. https://www.youtube.com/watch?v=ywj_sDnqQ1k

Palestinehumanrights. (2012e, November 24). *Protest Attack on Gaza in Auckland NZ 24 Nov 2012*. YouTube. https://www.youtube.com/watch?v=TnC4JsN2p3g.

Palestinehumanrights. (2013, May 16). *BDS of Apartheid Israel - Veolia Protest - Auckland NZ May 2015 [sic, 2013]*. YouTube. https://www.youtube.com/watch?v=EWm0nEzhHb8

Palestinehumanrights. (2014a, February 23). *Batsheva Dance Troupe Protest - Wellington New Zealand*. YouTube. https://www.youtube.com/watch?v=PhAAv-Q3pYE&t=41s

Palestinehumanrights. (2014b, July 19). *Marama Davidson speaks at Rally for Palestine/Gaza Auckland, Aotearoa New Zealand 19 Jul 2014*. YouTube. https://www.youtube.com/watch?v=Vw988GrELmQ

Palestinehumanrights. (2014c, July 19). *John Minto speaks at Gaza/Palestine Rally 19 Jul 2014*. YouTube. https://www.youtube.com/watch?v=x0sL7i9YWUU

Palestinehumanrights. (2014d, July 20). *Mike Treen speaks of Israeli Racism against Palestinians at Gaza/Palestine Rally - Auckland, Aotearo* [sic]. YouTube. https://www.youtube.com/watch?v=aZp8XUUssNs

Palestinehumanrights. (2014e, July 20). *Kennedy Graham MP Green Party speak at Gaza/Palestine Rally - Auckland, NZ 19 Jul 2014*. YouTube. https://www.youtube.com/watch?v=5DjlGLAygrw

Palestinehumanrights. (2014f, July 20). *Roger Fowler, Kia Ora Gaza speaks in solidarity at Gaza/Palestine Rally - Auckland, NZ 2014.* YouTube. https://www.youtube.com/watch?v=0qz%2D%2DeWsSfY

Palestinehumanrights. (2014g, July 26). *Joe Carolan - Unite Union speaks outside US Consulate at Gaza/Palestine Rally - Akl, NZ 26 Jul 2014* [Video]. YouTube. https://www.youtube.com/watch?v=K_9bulC8pGo

Palestinehumanrights. (2014h, July 26). *Syd Keepa CTU - Mana speaks in solidarity at Gaza/Palestine Rally - Auckland, Aotearoa, New Zealand* [Video]. YouTube. https://www.youtube.com/watch?v=BuRymIIOSuI

Palestinehumanrights. (2014i, July 26). *Catherine Delahunty MP Green Party speaks in solidarity at Gaza/Palestine Rally AKL NZ 26 Jul 2014.* YouTube. https://www.youtube.com/watch?v=RI0wNYzWUTE

Palestinehumanrights. (2014j, August 2). *Billy Hania speaks in solidarity at Gaza/Palestine Rally AKL, NZ 02 Aug 2014.* YouTube. https://www.youtube.com/watch?v=XLudxUUrFGg

Palestinehumanrights. (2014k, August 9). *John Minto at free Palestine Rally in Auckland Aotearoa, NZ 09.08.2014.* YouTube. https://www.youtube.com/watch?v=5sgKdo7gDus

Palestinehumanrights. (2014l, August 9). *Priyanca Radhakrishnan - Labour Party at Free Palestine Rally in Auckland Aotearoa, NZ 09.08.2014.* YouTube. https://www.youtube.com/watch?v=SCFNC7UGfTU

Palestinehumanrights. (2014m, August 16). *Welcome to Palestine rally in Auckland Aotearoa, NZ 16.08.2014.* YouTube. https://www.youtube.com/watch?v=LhiLX9TskDs.

Palestinehumanrights. (2014n, August 16). *David Shearer - Labour party at free Palestine Rally in Auckland Aotearoa, NZ 16.08.2014.* YouTube. https://www.youtube.com/watch?v=u-j0qdGjckg

Palestinehumanrights. (2014o, August 16). *Robert Reid - First Union speaks at Free Palestine Rally in Auckland Aotearoa, NZ 16.08.2014.* YouTube. https://www.youtube.com/watch?v=AxFSRcfbUKs

Palestinehumanrights. (2014p, August 16). *Palestine March in Auckland Aotearoa, NZ 16.08.2014.* YouTube. https://www.youtube.com/watch?v=VcPFM7Cavks

Palestinehumanrights. (2014q, August 23). *Tali Williams at Protest NZ Super Fund: Divest from Israel war machine: Downtown Auckland, NZ 23.08.14.* YouTube. https://www.youtube.com/watch?v=PkATVSlGPd8

Palestinehumanrights. (2016a, August 28). *NZ Rep MP Marama Davidson on the Women's Boat To Gaza speaks at fundraising dinner 2016 08 28 07 56.* YouTube. https://www.youtube.com/watch?v=jPEfUIFU7UQ

Palestinehumanrights. (2016b, September 21). *Women's Boat to Gaza- Green MP Marama Davidson.* YouTube. https://www.youtube.com/watch?v=q7grqLX1-9Q

Palestinehumanrights. (2016c, October 7). *Green MP Marama Davidson Welcomed at AKL, NZ Airport 08.10.2016 after Being Hijacked by Israeli Navy.* YouTube. https://www.youtube.com/watch?v=LBu9FMV1xVY

Palestinehumanrights. (2016d, November 8). *NZ Green Party MP Marama Davidson speaks out about Palestine & her experiences on WBG.* YouTube. https://www.youtube.com/watch?v=D7J3I_mVgrg

Palestinehumanrights. (2018a, February 14). *Gideon Levy public lecture, New Zealand, 2017.* YouTube. https://www.youtube.com/watch?v=CrZfPanKHcQ

Palestinehumanrights. (2018b, February 5). *Mike Treen National Director Unite Union New Zealand speaks at Palestine Free Ahed Tamimi Rally.* YouTube. https://www.youtube.com/watch?v=8K_hncUvKJk

Palestinehumanrights. (2018c, February 6). *Justine Sachs Dayenu - New Zealand speaks at Palestine Free Ahed Tamimi Rally.* YouTube. https://www.youtube.com/watch?v=-oJL3VekSkI

Palestinehumanrights. (2018d, February 6). *Roger Fowler - Kia Ora Gaza - New Zealand speaks at Palestine Free Ahed Tamimi Rally.* YouTube. https://www.youtube.com/watch?v=3Cm0Pi3Swss

Pettitt, R. T. (2015). Internal part political relationship marketing: Encouraging activism amongst local party members. In J. Lees-Marshment (Ed.), *Routledge handbook of political marketing* (pp. 137–150). Routledge.

PSNA. (2019, June 27). *Palestine Solidarity Network Aotearoa - Newsletter No 1* [Brochure].

SJP VUW - Students for Justice in Palestine: Victoria University of Wellington. (2017, December 16). *Dec 16: Palestine Picnic!* [Infographic]. Facebook. www.facebook.com/events/296748547500635/

Wellington Palestine. (n.d.). *About.* Retrieved May 12, 2018, from https://wellingtonpalestine.nz/about/

WPG (Wellington Palestine Group). (2016, August 28). *Letter to SuperFund (WPG)* [Press release]. http://www.palestinesolidaritynz.net/img/res_pdf/2016-08%20WPG%20NZ%20Superfund.pdf

CHAPTER 3

Israel Institute of New Zealand

Abstract This chapter analyses the political marketing, public diplomacy, and nation branding activities of the Israel Institute of New Zealand (IINZ), a Zionist think tank seeking to improve Israel's public image in New Zealand. It draws upon a content analysis of webpages, paraphernalia, social media posts, and audio-visual content produced by IINZ between 2010 and 2018. These primary sources were supplemented by an interview with David Cumin, one of IINZ's directors. This chapter will give a brief description of the Israel Institute before discussing the group's market-orientation, "segmentation, targeting, and position" (STP), internal marketing, public diplomacy, and nation branding strategies and activities.

Keywords Zionism • Anti-semitism • Sales-orientation • Segments • Base strategy • Public diplomacy

Overview

The Israel Institute of New Zealand is an Auckland-based think tank whose stated mission is to promote "a better understanding of the State of Israel through accurate analysis, insightful commentary, and effective

© The Author(s), under exclusive license to Springer Nature Switzerland AG 2022
A. Lim, *Political Marketing and Public Diplomacy by Pro-Israel and Pro-Palestinian Advocacy Groups*, Palgrave Studies in Political Marketing and Management,
https://doi.org/10.1007/978-3-031-15332-7_3

advocacy." The IINZ (n.d.) is led by three directors—Dr David Cumin, a University of Auckland anaesthesiology lecturer and member of Auckland's Jewish community; Ashley Church, CEO of the Property Institute of New Zealand; and Perry Trotter, an Auckland-based photographer, Christian Zionist, and creator of the Shadows of Shoah Holocaust exhibition. According to Cumin, the Israel Institute's formation was prompted by New Zealand's co-sponsorship of UN Security Council Resolution 2334 in December 2016, which condemned Israeli settlement expansion in the West Bank. Besides these three part-time directors, the Institute is also supported by several supporters and donors (IINZ, 2018b, 2018h). In addition to their online output, the IINZ has also organised some public functions, an opinion poll, and undertaken advocacy work.

Marketing Orientation

The author found that the IINZ pursued a sales-orientation, which involves using marketing intelligence to identify supporters and designing effective communications and activities to reach them (Lees-Marshment, 2004, 2014). Cumin (personal communication, March 3, 2020) confirmed that the Israel Institute conducted market intelligence in the form of public opinion polling and segmentation. The IINZ segmented its audience into two main segments: "the naïve and undecided" and "pro-Israel supporters" Since people in the 16–30 age demographic are less likely to support Israel and more sympathetic to the so-called "anti-Israel" groups, Cumin said that the IINZ had focused on creating a social media presence. Besides the Israel Institute's Facebook and Twitter channels, Cumin indicated that the Israel Institute was interested in expanding to other social media platforms such as Tik Tok, Snapchat and Instagram if they had more resources. Taken together, the content analysis and interview suggest that the Israel Institute conducted rudimentary segmentation and targeted a broad, pro-Israel audience but has also adapted its communications and relational methods such as social media and Māori culture to reach out to younger people and the Māori community. This shows that the Israel Institute has been able to adapt to meet the needs of certain segments.

This research found that the IINZ followed the five-stage process associated with sales-oriented charities, which is outlined in Table 3.1:

Table 3.1 The IINZ analysed using Lees-Marshment's sales-oriented framework

Stages	Definitions	Examples
Product design	Design a wide range of behaviour in accordance to what they think is right or works best.	Defending Israel, Zionism, and the New Zealand Jewish diaspora. Combating anti-Semitism and the BDS Movement (IINZ, n.d.).
Market intelligence	Identify the groups and segments of the public most likely to support it, using market segmentation to target them, and discuss how best to influence and persuade them.	Using public opinion surveys and segmenting its audience into the "undecided" and pro-Israel supporters. Using social media to reach out to younger people and cultural outreaches to Māori (IINZ, 2017a; S. Trotter, 2018; Cumin, personal communication, March 3, 2020).
Communication	Proactive, entertaining communication designed to attract attention, influence the public and civil society, raise income from potential supporters; using a wide range of marketing techniques such as pamphlets, posters, websites, Facebook, and Twitter.	Using its website (https://israelinstitute.nz), Facebook (https://www.facebook.com/Israel.Institute.NZ/), Twitter (https://twitter.com/IsraelInstNZ), and YouTube (https://www.youtube.com/channel/UCCunLRO6b9Z3JAlECtptLbQ) social media accounts, and an email newsletter called *The Advocate* to disseminate information (Cumin, personal communication, March 3, 2020).
Campaign	Short-term, one-off appeals	Meeting journalists and politicians, organising public events like the "Celebrate Israel at 70" rally, public opinion polls, producing voting guides, and soliciting donations (Cumin, personal communication, March 3, 2020; IINZ, 2017a, 2017b).
Delivery	Deliver what it thinks is best, promoting it in the most positive way possible.	Reporting its progress and achievements on its website, social media, and email newsletter including its substantial social media following and engagement with political elites.

Analysis

In terms of marketing orientation, the IINZ followed the five-stage process associated with sales-oriented advocacy groups. First, it has a product in the form of promoting Israel and Zionism and combating anti-Semitism and the BDS movement. Second, the IINZ has engaged in market intelligence by using a public opinion survey and targeted two major segments: the "naïve and undecided" and "pro-Israel supporters." Besides seeking to cultivate Māori support for Israel, the organisation has also used the Internet and social media to reach younger audiences. Third, the IINZ has disseminated its message on accessible, modern communications technologies such as the Internet, social media platforms, and email newsletters to maximise its outreach. Fourth, the IINZ has engaged in some short-term campaigns including a public opinion survey, voting guide, and fundraising. Finally, the Israel Institute has used its communications output and public opinion polls to inform its supporters about its achievements. The group's large social media following and engagement with political elites were regarded as successes in its advocacy work.

SEGMENTATION, TARGETING, AND POSITIONING (STP)

Segmentation

The Israel Institute followed all three stages of Bartle and Griffiths' (2002) "segmentation, targeting and, positioning" (STP) process. In July 2017, the think tank commissioned Curia Market Research to conduct a survey on New Zealand public opinion towards Israel. This survey drew upon a sample of 1000 New Zealanders. The IINZ's (2017a) survey found that:

- 55% of respondents supported Israel while 13% opposed Israel.
- Regarding New Zealand's co-sponsorship of UN Security Council Resolution 2334, 27% believed the New Zealand Government was right to co-sponsor the resolution, 30% believed that the Government should have abstained, and 43% were unsure.
- That 23% of female and 32% of men supported the New Zealand Government's decision to co-sponsor Resolution 2334. By contrast, 28% of women and 31% of men thought that New Zealand should have abstained from the resolution.

- That 37% of Wellingtonians believed that the New Zealand Government should have abstained from Resolution 2334. By contrast, 16% of Wellingtonians supported the Government's decision to co-sponsor the resolution.
- That 34% of Labour voters and 26% of Greens voters thought the New Zealand Government should have abstained from Resolution 2334. By contrast, 25% and 45% of Labour and Green voters supported the Government's decision to co-sponsor the resolution.
- That 60% of male and 51% of female respondents believed that Israel should exist as a "majority" Jewish state. By contrast, only 13% of male and 12% of female respondents disagreed with the idea that Israel should not exist as a majority Jewish state.
- That 58% of both the 18–30 years and over 60s age segments were most likely to support Israel as a majority Jewish State.
- That majority support for Israel's right to exist as a Jewish State existed across party lines: National (58%: 10%), New Zealand First (51%: 20%), and the Greens (56%: 21%).

Based on the survey, Cumin claimed "that support for Israel cuts across ages, genders, location and party lines" and that the New Zealand public was conflicted on the issue of how New Zealand should have responded to UN Resolution 2334. This survey showed that the Israel Institute is interested in conducting surveys and knows how to segment based on various categories including political affiliations, gender, regions, and attitudes towards Israel-related issues. As a form of market intelligence, the IINZ uses segmentation to identify key pro-Israel segments in New Zealand.

In addition to the 2017 survey, Cumin (personal communication, March 3, 2020) confirmed that the Israel Institute segmented its audience into two categories: "the naïve and undecided" and pro-Israel supporters. Based on the group's public opinion polling, Cumin claimed that public support for Israel cut across all ages, locations, and even political lines in New Zealand. However, the IINZ's polling found that the younger age demographic between 16 and 30 years were less likely to support Israel and more sympathetic to arguments and messaging of Palestinian solidarity groups. In response, the Israel Institute invested substantial time and resources into developing a social media presence via Facebook, Twitter, and YouTube. Thus, both the 2017 public opinion poll and Cumin's interview confirmed that the Israel Institute used public opinion polling to conduct segmentation in order to refine its targeting and positioning practices.

Targeting

Second, the Israel Institute targeted pro-Israel segments and the "undecided" within New Zealand society through its communications output and relational activities such as sponsoring the "Celebrate Israel at 70" rally in May 2018, film screenings and the 2018 Aotearoa-Israel Powhiri (Māori welcoming ceremony) (IINZ, 2018e; Shalom.Kiwi, 2018; S. Trotter, 2018). During an interview with Radio Shalom, Cumin identified the local Jewish and Christian communities as the strongest pillars of pro-Israel support in New Zealand (IINZ, 2018b). Jewish diasporic support for Israel would have been motivated by a desire to preserve relationships with Israel and the global Jewish diaspora. Within mainstream Jewish circles, Israel is viewed as the national homeland and protector of the Jewish people. In the case of pro-Israel Christians such as New Zealand National Party Member of Parliament Alfred Ngaro and C4Israel New Zealand National Director Bryce Turner, support for Israel is motivated by a desire for Judeo-Christian reconciliation in the wake of centuries of Christian anti-Semitism and persecution (P. Trotter, 2018c, 2018e). Other major factors have included Christian Zionist beliefs about the Jews being God's "Chosen People" and the restoration of Israel being a prelude to the Second Coming of Jesus Christ (McDowell et al., 2009; F. Shapiro, 2015).

Besides Jews and Christians, other pro-Israel segments in New Zealand have included Hindus and Baha'is. The Hindu segment was represented by the Indian Association's President Roy Kaunds, who voiced support for Israel on behalf of the New Zealand Hindu community (P. Trotter, 2018d; Celebrate Israel at 70 event, personal communication, May 13, 2018). Kaunds' presence reflects a sympathy for Israel within the Indian Hindu community and diaspora in response to Hindu-Muslim communal tensions and the antagonistic nature of Indo-Pakistani relations. In addition, Indo-Israel relations have also blossomed under the tenure of Indian Prime Minister Narendra Modi, leader of the Hindu nationalist Bharatiya Janata Party (BJP); which has led to networking between Zionist and Hindutva groups and advocates (Kumaraswamy, 2017; Sharma & Bing, 2015; Silverstein & Bazian, 2021; Therwath, 2007). Similarly, the pro-Israel sympathy of Baha'is reflects Israel's policy of religious tolerance, which favours the interests of their community. Haifa also hosts the Baha'i World Centre, which serves as the faith's headquarters (Heern, 2017; Lynfield, 2017). This analysis shows that the Israel Institute has a clear sense of pro-Israel segments within New Zealand and that it has forged relationships with key influencers and stakeholders within these communities who are able to mobilise support for their cause and interests.

Besides pro-Israel segments, the IINZ also targeted young people. During an interview with Radio Shalom, Cumin expressed concern "that the youth growing up have not had the more balanced perspective that there was in the past. Correcting that should be what we are mindful of" (IINZ, 2018b). When interviewed by the author, Cumin (personal communication, March 3, 2020) stated that the Israel Institute was interested in using social media platforms to reach out to the 16–30 age demographic, who were less likely to support Israel and more receptive to the messaging and arguments of Palestinian solidarity groups.

The intergenerational gap in public perceptions of Israel reflects the growing international scrutiny of Israeli policies and actions towards the Palestinians. While many in the older generations regarded Israel as a plucky young nation fighting for its survival, many in the younger generations view Israel as a "Goliath" that is oppressing the Palestinians. Taken together, these interviews confirm that younger audiences in New Zealand are a key target of the Israel Institute's communications and advocacy work.

Positioning

Third, the Israel Institute conducted "psychological positioning" to manage Israel's public image in New Zealand. Whereas "real positioning" seeks to alter the product to cater for the market, psychological positioning focuses on altering perceptions of their product (Bartle & Griffiths, 2002). The organisation was primarily concerned with combating negative perceptions of Israel and promoting sympathy and understanding for Israel within New Zealand. The Israel Institute has promoted several pro-Israel messages and narratives including:

- Israel being a vibrant, pluralistic democracy and advanced society (Bing, 2018).

- Israel wanting peace while the Palestinians seeking Israel's destruction (P. Trotter, 2017b).
- Attributing the Palestinian refugee problem, restrictions on Palestinians, and the Gaza Blockade to both Palestinian anti-Semitism and hostility towards Israel (P. Trotter, 2016a, 2016b).
- Claiming that mainstream media and United Nations are biased against Israel (Bayefsky, 2017; IINZ, 2018c).
- Claiming that Palestinian advocates such as the BDS Movement and Kia Ora Gaza are anti-Semitic movements seeking to delegitimise and destroy Israel (Cumin, 2018a; S. Trotter, 2017a).
- Framing Zionism as an indigenous rights movement seeking to restore the Jews to their historical homeland (P. Trotter, 2017a).
- Presenting Zionism and the State of Israel as integral elements of Jewish identity, culture, and history. While the IINZ does accept that the State of Israel does make mistakes, they oppose efforts by Palestinian solidarity advocates and groups to distinguish between anti-Semitism and anti-Zionism; regarding anti-Zionism as the latest manifestation of anti-Semitism (Shalom.Kiwi, 2017c; P. Trotter, 2018b).

Taken together, the Israel Institute seeks to present Israel as the victim of Palestinian aggression and a hostile international community and mainstream media that are biased against Israel. In addition, the Israel Institute seeks to reframe Zionism and the State of Israel as legitimate expressions of Jewish identity and aspirations. These messages and narratives underpin the Israel Institute's worldview, which are shared by many Zionist advocates and groups in Israel and the global Jewish diaspora.

In addition, a content analysis of the IINZ's web and social media output found that the group also positioned their cause and messages at the Māori community. Some examples of Māori-oriented positioning activities have included:

- Promoting pro-Israel Māori figures such as IINZ contributor Sheree Trotter, Pastor Tawhiri Littlejohn, New Zealand National Party MP Ngaro, and businessman Arama Kukutai. During the Celebrate Israel at 70 event, Trotter and Littlejohn sought to link Māori indigeneity to Jewish indigeneity to Israel by asserting that Māori and Jews were able to trace their historical connection to their homelands through their *whakapapa* (or genealogies). Reflecting his Christian Zionist worldview, Ngaro also likened the Treaty of Waitangi to the Biblical

Abrahamic Covenant, which in the Judeo-Christian view established Jews as God's "Chosen People" (P. Trotter, 2018c, 2018f)
- Highlighting Kukutai's efforts to facilitate cooperation and the exchange of information and technology between the New Zealand and Israeli agricultural sectors (Cumin, 2018f).
- Organising Māori-themed pro-Israel events such as the Aotearoa-Israel Powhiri. Besides serving as a show of strength by pro-Israel New Zealanders, the Powhiri would also showcase Māori culture and arts (S. Trotter, 2018).
- Producing a video featuring a Samoan Māori man criticising the BDS Movement (P. Trotter, 2018a). This seeks to combat Palestinian solidarity advocates' efforts to reach the Māori and Pasifika communities.

Through these Māori-oriented positioning activities, the IINZ hopes to counter the inroads made into that community by Māori pro-Palestinian figures such as Marama Davidson and Hone Harawira. While Palestinian advocates sought to draw a parallel between Māori and Palestinian experiences with colonisation and land loss, the IINZ and other pro-Israel advocates have emphasised the commonality between Māori and Jewish indigeneity. Cumin (personal communication, 2020, July 28) later clarified that the Israel Institute had established contacts with several communities including Māori and took a particular interest in connecting with the Māori Christians, a pro-Israel sub-grouping. Taken together, these findings show that the Israel Institute uses culturally specific methods to reach out to certain demographics.

Analysis

The IINZ followed all three stages of the "segmentation, targeting, and positioning" process. First, the organisation conducted public opinion polling for the purpose of identifying segments and gauging public opinion. Cumin confirmed that the IINZ segmented their audience into pro-Israel supporters and the "undecided." Second, the IINZ targeted various pro-Israel segments through a range of communications output and relational activities. While key pro-Israel segments have included the Jewish and Christian communities, the IINZ was also interested in other segments including Hindus, Bahais, and young people. Social media was used to connect with the younger generation. Third, the IINZ conducted psychological positioning by using arguments and narratives casting Israel and Zionism in a positive light. The organisation also sought to win over the Māori community by using pro-Israel Māori figures, culture, and arts to appeal to Māori Christians. In short, the IINZ had the ability to identify segments and to allocate resources and activities to reaching them. Sometimes the messaging and medium was tailored when targeting certain ethnic and religious segments.

Internal Marketing

While the content analysis yielded no information about the Israel Institute's internal marketing, Cumin (personal communication, 2020, March 3) confirmed that the group sought to promote a sense of belonging among its subscribers by reaching out to thank them for their support. In addition, the IINZ pursued a broader strategy of publicising their advocacy work and achievements on their website, social media, and email newsletters including their efforts to hold New Zealand officials and media to account for policies and coverage deemed unfriendly to Israel. Cumin also mentioned that the IINZ had plans to establish a network of "friends of the Institute" groups across New Zealand to facilitate a sense of belonging and provide educational material. The interview findings suggest that the Israel Institute pursues a base strategy which involves "giving stakeholders what they want" (Pettitt, 2015, pp. 143–144). Due to its Zionist orientation, the group would naturally attract people who are sympathetic to defending Israel and Zionism's image in New Zealand.

A base strategy also works well with a sales-oriented advocacy group which focuses on selling its product to the wider public instead of designing a product that would fit with what the public wants or needs. While supporters of Israel remain a key audience, the Israel Institute has adapted its communications and relational activities to reaching certain segments like youth and Māori, as discussed above.

Analysis

The IINZ has met the criteria of internal marketing by pursuing a base strategy. As a Zionist cause group, the Israel Institute has pursued a base strategy by keeping its supporters informed of its efforts to promote a favourable image of Israel in New Zealand, thus appealing to their affinity and support for Israel.

Public Diplomacy and Nation Branding

The Israel Institute has also conducted informal public diplomacy and nation branding to help manage Israel's public image in New Zealand through a range of communicational and relational activities. These have included working with foreign officials including diplomats and policy-makers; producing informational content that promoted Israel in a positive light and combated negative imagery and hostility towards Israel; and promoting pro-Israel public gatherings and politically oriented tourism.

Working with Foreign Officials and Governments

First, the Israel Institute has cultivated relationships with several veteran Israeli policy-makers including the former Israeli negotiator Moty Cristal, former Israeli Labor Party politician Einat Wilf, and the dissident Palestinian journalist Bassam Eid. These individuals participated in video interviews covering the Oslo peace process, Zionism, the Palestinian leadership, and BDS Movement (P. Trotter, 2016b, 2017a). Besides giving their audience access to Israeli perspectives, hosting these Israeli officials helped the IINZ to gain access to key policy-makers within the Israeli political establishment who are sympathetic to their pro-Israel advocacy work. In addition, hosting a Palestinian dissident such as Eid lends legitimacy to Zionist criticism of the Palestinian leadership and BDS Movement at least within pro-Israel circles.

In addition to these individual contacts, the Israel Institute has also forged institutional contacts with the Israeli Government. In mid-March 2018, the IINZ participated in the 6th Global Forum for Combating Anti-Semitism in Jerusalem, which was hosted by the Israeli Ministry of Foreign Affairs and the Ministry of Diaspora Affairs. Cumin and Perry Trotter represented the Israel Institute. The conference was attended by a thousand delegates from Israel and 83 countries including the Australia/Israel & Jewish Affairs' (AIJAC's) Director of International and Community Affairs Jeremy Jones, Israeli Deputy Foreign Minister Tzipi Hotovely, the British Chief Rabbi Ephraim Mirvis, Executive Vice Chairman of the Conference of Presidents of Major American Jewish Organizations Malcolm Hoenlein, former French Prime Minister Manuel Valls, Jewish Agency chairman Nathan Sharansky, and senior clergy from the Jewish, Catholic, and Muslim communities. The conference focused on efforts by governments and civil society actors to combat anti-Semitism and Holocaust denial. During the Global Forum, the Israeli, Greek, Maltese and Italian justice ministers also signed a "Joint Statement on Countering Online Hate Speech and Incitement to Violence and Terrorism" focusing on hate speech, violence, and terror incitement on social media. Reflecting Facebook's cooperation with the Israeli Government in deleting terrorism-related content, Delphine Reyer, the company's Policy Director for the Southern Africa, Middle East, and Africa Region, attended the signing ceremony. The Joint Statement reflects a willingness of governments and non-state actors such as multinational corporations (MNCs) to collaborate on issues of shared interests such as hate speech and counter-terrorism. As a state-sponsored event, the Global Forum seeks to coordinate efforts by the Israeli Government, civil society groups, and business actors to combat anti-Semitism on an international level (Cumin, 2018c; Kutner, 2018). The IINZ's participation in the Global Forum shows that it is part of a global pro-Israel "transnational advocacy network" of NGOs which supports Israeli public diplomacy efforts including combating anti-Semitism.

Communicational Output

In terms of communicational activities, the Israel Institute has produced articles and videos promoting Israel in a positive light and combating negative imagery and publicity around Israel. First, the IINZ has promoted positive stories about Israel:

- The *Lancet* medical journal editor Richard Horton's efforts to make amends for the journal's previous anti-Israel content by publishing a special issue focusing on Israel's health achievements (Cumin, 2017). This morale-boosting article would highlight a victory in the global struggle against the BDS campaign, which Israel advocates regard as the latest manifestation of anti-Semitism.
- IINZ contributor Sheree Trotter (S. Trotter, 2017b) discussed the centenary of the Balfour Declaration, focusing on how it facilitated the re-establishment of the Jewish homeland.
- Shalom.Kiwi founder and guest contributor IINZ Moses (2017) defended New Zealand's participation in the Middle East theatre of World War I on the grounds it ended Ottoman rule and facilitated the restoration of Israel.

- Karl du Fresne (2018) has argued that Israel is a success story, describing Israel as an "oasis of democracy." While acknowledging that transgressions have occurred on the Israeli side such as the Sabra and Shatila massacres and Baruch Goldstein's massacre of 29 Palestinian worshippers in 1995, du Fresne highlighted Israel's willingness to make peace and the threat of Hezbollah and Hamas. He also defended the Trump Administration's relocation of the US Embassy to Jerusalem as a recognition of the importance of Jerusalem to Jewish history, culture, and religion.
- Covering a bilateral innovation agreement with Israel, publicising Israeli digital technology and joint Israeli-New Zealand agritech cooperation (Cumin, 2018d; IINZ, 2018a, 2018d).

The IINZ has published these articles and videos to combat a perceived deficit of positive stories about Israel in the New Zealand media. The IINZ also highlights what it regards as victories for Israel such as *The Lancet's* efforts to make amends for anti-Israel content and efforts to deepen New Zealand's economic and technological engagement with Israel. In addition, the Israel Institute also highlights historical developments such as the Balfour Declaration and World War I, framing them as steps that led to the "re-establishment" of Israel. In response to the negative imagery associated with war and occupation, the IINZ also seeks to portray Israel as a democracy and technologically innovative country.

Secondly, the IINZ has also produced articles and videos to counter negative imagery and publicity around Israeli policies and actions:

- Criticising political figures including Green co-leader Marama Davidson, TOP leader Gareth Morgan and former Foreign Minister Murray McCully for pursuing policies and actions deemed to be hostile towards Israel (Bell, 2017; Shalom.Kiwi, 2017a; S. Trotter, 2017a).
- Criticising the deletion of references to Israel in Artsplash's *Joseph and the Amazing Technicolor Dreamcoat* musical (Shalom. Kiwi, 2017b).
- Challenging several media outlets including Radio New Zealand, the *New Zealand Herald*, the *Otago Daily Times*, Newshub, and Stuff for their alleged inaccurate coverage of Israeli cross-border operations into Syria after an Iranian drone penetrated Israeli airspace (IINZ, 2018c).

- During the 2018 Gaza March of Return, the IINZ welcomed public broadcaster Television New Zealand's (TVNZ) acknowledgement that it had exaggerated the Palestinian death toll (IINZ, 2018g). IINZ also challenged Annabelle Lee, the executive producer of Newshub's *The Hui* current affairs show, for retweeting a Twitter post claiming that Israel had exploited the trauma of the Holocaust to justify its oppression of millions of Palestinians (Benson, 2018; IINZ, 2018h).
- Sharing external pro-Israel video content including a UN Watch video criticising the Palestinian Liberation Organisation (PLO) for inciting hatred against Israel and an Israeli Defence Forces (IDF) video about the 2018 Gaza Land March (UN Watch, 2017; "British-born IDF major honoured with award for contribution to Israel," 2018; Cumin, 2018b). The UN Watch video featured Palestinian dissident Mosab Hassan Yousef as a pro-Israel Palestinian voice who helped lend legitimacy to Israeli criticism of the PLO and Palestinian Authority. Meanwhile, the presence of British-born Major Keren Hajioff in the IDF video articulated the interlocking messages that Israeli society empowers women and the unbreakable bond between the Jewish Diaspora and State of Israel.

These articles and videos show that the IINZ has challenged political leaders, the media, and entertainment sectors for promoting alleged negative and inaccurate information about Israel. Besides combating perceived efforts to isolate and denigrate Israel, the Israel Institute has also sought to defend Israel's conduct in conflicts such as the 2018 Gaza Land March. The use of external video content shows that the IINZ sees itself as working with like-minded allies on a global level to defend Israel. In short, the IINZ's communicational image management output reinforces Israel public diplomacy and nation branding messages and narratives.

Relational Activities

In terms of relational activities, the Israel Institute has promoted pro-Israel public gatherings and politically oriented tourism. These activities promote Israeli and Jewish culture, heritage, and identity, and tourism to Israel while combating negative perceptions of Israel in response to the Israel-Palestine conflict.

The IINZ has promoted several public gatherings in support of Israeli public diplomacy and nation branding efforts:

- The IINZ participated in a series of pro-Israel gatherings across New Zealand called the "New Zealand Bless Israel Celebration" in late April 2018. The New Zealand Celebration was organised by Christian Zionist leader Jane Troughton as part of a series of global Christian Zionist gatherings to express solidarity with Israel and promote Jewish-Christian reconciliation. Besides Auckland and other major cities, gatherings were also held in provincial towns like Mosgiel, Wainuiomata, Papamoa, Kaiwaka, Levin, and Gore. Notable attendees included the Israeli Ambassador Itzhak Gerbeg, New Zealand National Party MP Ngaro, NZJC spokesperson Julie Moses, and IINZ co-director David Cumin (Shalom.Kiwi, 2018). Gerbeg's presence in his official capacity as Ambassador reflects the Israeli Embassy's efforts to network with local Jewish and Christian Zionist groups.
- The "Celebrate Israel at 70" was a rally held in Auckland in May 2018 to commemorate the 70th anniversary of Israel's independence. This rally attracted pro-Israel supporters from the Jewish, Christian, Māori, Pasifika, Indian, and Hindu communities including Ngati Whatua representative and Pastor Tawhiri Littlejohn, New Zealand National Party MP Ngaro, Indian Association spokesperson Roy Kaunds, Habonim Dror representatives Neveh Shimi and Alana Jacobson-Pepere, Christians for Israel New Zealand (C4Israel) National Director Bryce Turner, and Zionist Federation leader Rob Berg (IINZ, 2018e). These speakers articulated several pro-Israel messages highlighting Israel's democratic credentials, right to self-defence, the "unbreakable bond" between Israel and the Jewish diaspora, Jewish indigeneity, commitment to minorities' human rights, and Israeli technological and scientific innovation (P. Trotter, 2018c, 2018f; Celebrate Israel at 70 event, personal communication, May 13, 2018). Their messages and arguments reflected Israeli public diplomacy and nation branding efforts aimed at highlighting Israel's legitimacy and the Jewish historical connection to what they regarded as their "ancestral homeland." In response, 30 pro-Palestinian Auckland Peace Action counterdemonstrators picketed the rally, staging a "Wall of Noise" (Bhattarai, 2018). Conversely, Palestinian solidarity advocates regarded the Celebrate Israel at 70 as a platform

for Israeli hasbara and Zionist propaganda aimed at erasing and vilifying the Palestinians.
- Covering the screening of Israeli film director Yariv Mozer's film *Ben Gurion, Epilogue* at the 13th Doc Edge Film Festival in Wellington and Auckland in May 2018, which was sponsored by the Israeli Embassy (IINZ, 2018f).
- Covering the Aotearoa-Israel Powhiri in July 2018, a special welcoming ceremony organised for Israeli Ambassador Itzhak Gerbeg and Honorary Consul David Robinson by Ngaphui kaumatua (elder) Pat Ruka and other pro-Israel elements within the Māori community as a symbolic apology for New Zealand's co-sponsorship of UN Resolution 2334. The Powhiri showcased several Māori cultural elements including the Wero (a challenge to determine whether visitors come in peace or hostility), the Karanga (call onto the Marae), Mihi (speeches), Waiata (song) and performances by Hoani Waititi Kura Kapa Haka group and Pacific Pearls. In addition, members of the Auckland Jewish community sang Hebrew songs in honour of the guests (S. Trotter, 2018).

The Israel Institute has used these public gatherings to promote Israel in favourable light and facilitate cooperation with other pro-Israel segments in New Zealand society particularly Christian Zionists. Besides highlighting public support for Israel in New Zealand, public gatherings such as the "New Zealand Bless Israel Celebration" and "Celebrate Israel at 70" were used to articulate pro-Israel arguments and messages, thus advancing Israel public diplomacy and nation branding efforts. In addition, the IINZ has assisted Israeli public diplomacy by supporting the screening of Israeli films and forging ties with New Zealand civil society. The presence of the Israeli Ambassador Gerbeg at several of the events suggests a tacit official endorsement of the work carried out by pro-Israel advocacy groups in New Zealand. The presence of pro-Israel Māori individuals such as Pastor Littlejohn and Māori cultural elements at the Aotearoa-Israel Powhiri show that the Israel Institute has identified the Māori community as an important segment to win over.

Second, the IINZ has also promoted tourism to Israel as a means of improving public perceptions of Israel and fostering interpersonal relations between New Zealanders and Israelis. In mid-March 2018, the group published a Vimeo video of Cumin's (2018e) tour of four popular tourist destinations in Jerusalem: the Mahane Yehuda Market, the Knesset,

Mamilla Mall, and Jaffa Gate. Besides educating viewers about the historical significance of these sites and Israeli heritage preservation efforts, Cumin supported the Israeli Government's claim to Jerusalem as its "indivisible" capital. Finally, Cumin compared the Israeli presence favourably to the brief Jordanian occupation of Jerusalem between 1948 and 1967. While the Jordanians excluded Jews from East Jerusalem, the Israelis opened it to everyone again including adherents of all three Abrahamic faiths. Besides articulating pro-Israel arguments and messages, Cumin's video encouraged tourism to Jerusalem, thus supporting Israeli nation branding efforts to emphasise the city's cultural and political importance to Israel and Jews.

Analysis

The Israel Institute has engaged in informal public diplomacy and nation branding by supporting Israel's efforts to manage its international image and interests in New Zealand through various communicational and relational activities. First, the IINZ has cultivated relations with Israeli diplomats and officials. It has also participated in official Israeli Government functions such as the 6th Global Forum for combating anti-Semitism; which brings together both Israeli government and Zionist civil society actors. Second, the IINZ has produced or shared literature and media that promotes favourable messages and arguments about Israel while combating criticism and negative coverage of Israel. Fourth, the Israel Institute has sponsored various pro-Israel public gatherings and encouraged politically oriented tourism to Israel. Finally, the IINZ also used its communicational output and relational activities to emphasise the importance of Israel to Jewish culture, heritage, and identity.

This case study shows that civil society actors can still support official public diplomacy and nation branding despite not being formally connected to governments. The Israel Institute appears to be part of a global pro-Israel transnational advocacy network where Zionist activists, groups, and state actors work together to advance Israeli interests and aspirations through advocacy and public diplomacy.

Conclusion

This chapter analysed the communications and advocacy activities of the Israel Institute of New Zealand against the researcher's political marketing and public diplomacy framework. The IINZ met most of the criteria of this framework. First in terms of market-orientation, the Israel Institute has followed the five stages of a sales-oriented charity. First, the IINZ has sought to promote Israel and Zionism and combat anti-Semitism and the BDS movement. Second, the IINZ has conducted public opinion polls and used segmentation to target young people and Māori via social media and the utilisation of Māori culture and pro-Israel personalities. Third, the IINZ has used the Internet, social media, and relational activities to reach a New Zealand audience. Fourth, the IINZ has engaged in some short-term campaigns with the goals of gauging New Zealand public sentiment towards Israel, influencing voting behaviour, and soliciting funds from sympathetic listeners. Finally, the Israel Institute has used its website, social media platforms, and email newsletters to inform its supporters about its achievements and progress.

Second, the IINZ followed all three stages of the "segmentation, targeting, and positioning" (STP) process. Both the content analysis and a follow-up interview with Cumin demonstrated that the Israel Institute used public opinion polling to segment their audience into both pro-Israel supporters and the "undecided." The organisation also targeted a wider range of segments based on ethnic, religious, and age groups. Different arguments and methods were used to reach different segments. Finally, the Israel Institute conducted psychological positioning by framing history and contemporary developments in Israel-Palestine through Zionist arguments and messages. The organisation also sought to win over the Māori community by using pro-Israel Māori figures, culture, and arts to appeal to that demographic. These findings show that the IINZ knows how to identify pro-Israel segments and how to tailor its messaging and activities to reaching them.

Third, the IINZ met the criteria of internal marketing by using ideological incentives to encourage activists and members to carry out external communications and relational activities. Pettitt's base strategy was the most relevant internal marketing model since it supported the research findings that the IINZ designed its product around the needs and expectations of its pro-Israel internal stakeholders. As part of its base strategy, the IINZ informed supporters about its efforts to defend Israel's image in

New Zealand, thus appealing to their pro-Israel sympathy. As a theory, a base strategy is useful for explaining how a cause-oriented group uses ideological commitment as the glue that binds together its support base.

Fourth, the IINZ practised informal public diplomacy and nation branding by managing Israel's public image in New Zealand. The think tank has cultivated relations with Israeli officials, networked with other Zionist activists and groups on a global level, and participated in official Israeli Government-sponsored functions. In addition, the Israel Institute has produced pro-Israel literature and media content, sponsored various pro-Israel events in New Zealand, and encouraged tourism to Israel. Besides promoting a favourable image of Israel and combating negative perceptions and media coverage, the IINZ has emphasised the Jewish historical and cultural connection to Israel.

References

Bartle, J., & Griffiths, D. (2002). Social-psychological, economic and marketing models of voting behaviour compared. In N. J. O'Shaughnessy & S. C. M. Henneberg (Eds.), *The idea of political marketing* (pp. 19–37). Praeger.

Bayefsky, A. (2017, January 3). *Is the UN fair to Israel*. IINZ. https://israelinstitute.nz/2017/01/is-the-un-fair-to-israel/

Bell, M. (2017, April 24). *Peter slams McCully over UN Resolution 2334*. IINZ. https://israelinstitute.nz/2017/04/peters-slams-mccully-over-un-resolution-2334/

Benson, P. (2018, July 19). *Talk show producer tweets hooey and why it matters*. Honest Reporting. https://honestreporting.com/tag/annabelle-lee/

Bhattarai, R. (2018, May 13). NZ pro-Palestinian 'justice' protesters target Israel Day waterfront events. *Asia Pacific Report*. https://asiapacificreport.nz/2018/05/13/nz-pro-palestinian-justice-protesters-target-israel-day-waterfront-events/

Bing, D. (2018, February 8). *Israel's history part 1 – The indigenous Jewish presence in Israel/Palestine*. IINZ. https://israelinstitute.nz/2018/02/israels-history-part-1-the-indigenous-jewish-presence-in-israel-palestine/

British-born IDF major honoured with award for contribution to Israel. (2018, May 2). *Jewish News*. http://jewishnews.timesofisrael.com/british-born-idf-major-honoured-with-award-for-contribution-to-israel/

Cumin, D. (2017, September 26). *Anti-Israel propaganda reversed in leading medical journal*. IINZ. https://israelinstitute.nz/2017/09/anti-israel-propaganda-reversed-in-leading-medical-journal/

Cumin, D. (2018a, January 23). *The seven serious BDS flaws*. IINZ. https://israelinstitute.nz/2018/01/the-seven-serious-bds-flaws/#BDS_lies

Cumin, D. (2018b, April 1). *The violent riots on the Gaza border*. IINZ. https://israelinstitute.nz/2018/04/the-violent-riots-on-the-gaza-border/.

Cumin, D. (2018c, April 4). *6th global forum for combating antisemitism*. IINZ. https://israelinstitute.nz/2018/04/6th-global-forum-for-combating-antisemitism/

Cumin, D. (2018d, April 29). *Israel and New Zealand cooperating in Agritech*. IINZ. https://israelinstitute.nz/2018/04/israel-and-new-zealand-cooperating-in-agritech/

Cumin, D. (2018e, March 24). *Four spots in Jerusalem*. IINZ – Israel Institute of New Zealand. https://israelinstitute.nz/2018/03/four-spots-in-jerusalem/

Cumin, D. (2018f, May 6). *Arama Kukutai on Israeli Agritech and NZ opportunities*. IINZ. https://israelinstitute.nz/2018/05/arama-kukutai-on-israel-agritech-and-nz-opportunities/

du Fresne, K. (2018, July 14). *Israel's continued existence a remarkable feat of survival*. IINZ. https://israelinstitute.nz/2018/07/israels-continuing-existence-a-remarkable-feat-of-survival/

Heern, Z.M. (2017, December 1). *Who are the Baha'is and why are they so persecuted?*. The Conversation. https://theconversation.com/who-are-the-bahais-and-why-are-they-so-persecuted-84042

IINZ. (2017a, August 9). *Strong Kiwi support for Israel: Israel Institute of New Zealand poll*. https://israelinstitute.nz/2017/08/strong-kiwi-support-israel-iinz-poll/

IINZ. (2017b, September 1). *IINZ Voters' Guide 2017*. https://israelinstitute.nz/voters-guide/

IINZ. (2018a, January 8). *Dr Cumin quoted in AIJAC article calling on NZ to acknowledge Jerusalem as Israel's capital*. http://web.archive.org/web/20180226093139/https://israelinstitute.nz/sideroom/dr-cumin-quoted-in-aijac-article-calling-on-nz-to-acknowledge-jerusalem-as-israels-capital/

IINZ. (2018b, February 4). *Radio Shalom interviews Dr Cumin*. http://web.archive.org/web/20180215115928/https://israelinstitute.nz/sideroom/radio-shalom-interviews-dr-cumin/

IINZ. (2018c, February 12). *New Zealand headlines mislead on Iranian provocation*. https://israelinstitute.nz/2018/02/new-zealand-headlines-mislead-on-iranian-provocation/

IINZ. (2018d, March 5). *Israeli leaders share success secrets with Kiwis*. https://israelinstitute.nz/2018/03/israeli-leaders-share-success-secrets-with-kiwis/

IINZ. (2018e, May 14). *Kiwis celebrate Israel's 70th birthday*. https://israelinstitute.nz/2018/05/kiwis-celebrate-israels-70th-birthday/

IINZ. (2018f, May 29) *Māori honour Ben Gurion film-maker* [Video]. https://israelinstitute.nz/2018/05/maori-honour-ben-gurion-film-maker/

IINZ. (2018g, July 12). *TVNZ admits inaccuracy in reporting on Gaza riots.* https://israelinstitute.nz/2018/07/tvnz-admits-inaccuracy-in-reporting-on-gaza-riots/

IINZ. (2018h, July 25). *J-Air interviewed Dr Cumin.* https://israelinstitute.nz/sideroom/j-air-interviewed-dr-cumin/

IINZ. (n.d.) *About.* Retrieved June 25, 2018. https://israelinstitute.nz/about/

Kumaraswamy, P. R. (2017). Redefining 'strategic' cooperation. *Strategic Analysis, 41*(4), 355–368. https://doi.org/10.1080/09700161.2017.1330451

Kutner, M. (2018, March 23). *Combating anti-Semitism.* IINZ. https://israelinstitute.nz/2018/03/combating-antisemitism/

Lees-Marshment, J. (2004). *The political marketing revolution: Transforming the government of the UK.* Manchester University Press.

Lees-Marshment, J. (2014). *Political marketing: Principles and applications* (2nd ed.). Routledge.

Lynfield, B. (2017, October 21). From their headquarters in Haifa, Baha'is seek to unify humanity. *The Jerusalem Post.* https://www.jpost.com/Israel-News/From-their-Haifa-headquarters-Bahais-seek-to-unite-humanity-508037

McDowell, D., Church, P., Tollestrup, S., Chapman, S., & Yule, R. (2009). *Israel: 5 views on people, land and state.* Vision Network of New Zealand.

Moses, J. (2017, November 9). *Israel a triumph over imperialism and adversity.* IINZ. https://israelinstitute.nz/2017/11/israel-a-triumph-over-imperialism-and-adversity/

Pettitt, R. T. (2015). Internal part political relationship marketing: Encouraging activism amongst local party members. In J. Lees-Marshment (Ed.), *Routledge handbook of political marketing* (pp. 137–150). Routledge.

Shalom.Kiwi. (2017a, March 3). *Did Gareth Morgan just excuse terrorism and anti-Semitism?.* IINZ. https://israelinstitute.nz/2017/03/did-gareth-morgan-just-excuse-terrorism-and-anti-semitism/

Shalom.Kiwi (2017b, June 30). *Censorship and the amazing bigotry of Artsplash.* IINZ. https://israelinstitute.nz/2017/06/censorship-and-the-amazing-bigotry-of-artsplash/

Shalom.Kiwi. (2017c, September 17). *The problem with Ardern's Corbyn endorsement.* IINZ. https://israelinstitute.nz/2017/09/jacinda-ardern-shows-poor-judgement/

Shalom.Kiwi. (2018, May 8). *New Zealanders show support for Israel.* IINZ. https://israelinstitute.nz/2018/05/new-zealanders-show-support-for-israel/

Shapiro, F. L. (2015). *Christian Zionism: Navigating the Jewish-Christian border.* Cascade Books.

Sharma, A. and Bing, D. (2015). India–Israel relations: the evolving partnership. *Israel Affairs* 21(4), 620–632 https://doi.org/10.1080/13537121.2015.1076189.

Silverstein, R. & Bazian, H. (2021, August). *Israel, India and the Islamophobic Alliance*. Islamophobia Studies Center. https://iphobiacenter.org/wp-content/uploads/2021/08/Israel-India-and-the-Islamophobic-Alliance.pdf

Therwath, I. (2007). Working for India or against Islam? Islamophobia in Indian American lobbies. *South Asia Multidisciplinary Academic Journal, 1*, 1–17. https://doi.org/10.4000/samaj.262

Trotter, P. (2016a, July 3). *A palestinian perspective*. IINZ. https://israelinstitute.nz/2016/07/a-palestinian-perspective/

Trotter, P. (2016b, July 23). *An insider's view: Negotiator Moty Cristal*. IINZ. https://israelinstitute.nz/2016/07/an-insiders-view-negotiator-moty-cristal/

Trotter, P. (2017a, July 15). *Einat Wilf: Zionism is an indigenous movement*. IINZ. https://israelinstitute.nz/2017/07/einat-wilf-zionism-indigenous-movement/

Trotter, S. (2017a, February 1). *Not all Māori on board with Marama*. IINZ. https://israelinstitute.nz/2017/02/not-all-maori-on-board-with-marama/

Trotter, P. (2017b, August 7). *A Jewish New Zealander's view on Israel*. IINZ. https://israelinstitute.nz/2017/08/i-am-a-zionist/

Trotter, S. (2017b, October 27). *The Balfour declaration at the ends of the earth*. IINZ. https://israelinstitute.nz/2017/10/the-balfour-declaration-at-the-ends-of-the-earth/

Trotter, S. (2018, August 1). *Historic Māori-led apology to Israel*. IINZ. https://israelinstitute.nz/2018/08/historic-maori-led-apology-to-israel/

Trotter, P. (2018a, January 26). *A Samoan Maori on BDS*. IINZ. https://israelinstitute.nz/2018/01/a-samoan-maori-on-bds/

Trotter, P. (2018b, April 18). *A feminist and a Zionist*. IINZ. https://israelinstitute.nz/2018/04/a-feminist-and-a-zionist/

Trotter, P. (2018c, May 15). *Hon Alfred Ngaro: Celebrating Israel at 70*. IINZ. https://israelinstitute.nz/2018/05/hon-alfred-ngaro-celebrating-israel-at-70/

Trotter, P. (2018d, May 16). *Roy Kaunds of India Assoc of NZ at Celebrate Israel 70*. IINZ. https://israelinstitute.nz/2018/05/roy-kaunds-of-india-assoc-of-nz-at-celebrate-israel-70/

Trotter, P. (2018e, May 16). *C4I's Bryce Turner at Celebrate Israel at 70*. IINZ. https://israelinstitute.nz/2018/05/bryce-turner-of-c4i-at-celebrate-israel-at-70/

Trotter, P. (2018f, May 17). *We the Māori people, support Israel*. IINZ. https://israelinstitute.nz/2018/05/we-the-maori-people-support-israel/

UN Watch. (2017, September 28). *Palestinian exposes lies at UN*. IINZ. https://israelinstitute.nz/2017/09/palestinian-exposes-lies-at-un/

CHAPTER 4

Australia/Israel & Jewish Affairs Council

Abstract This chapter analyses the political marketing, public diplomacy, and nation branding activities of the Australia/Israel & Jewish Affairs Council (AIJAC), a pro-Israel Australian Jewish think tank and advocacy group. It draws upon a content analysis of webpages, magazine articles, op-ed columns, videos, and social media posts produced by AIJAC between 2010 and 2018. These primary sources were supplemented by several external sources that filled several gaps encountered during the content analysis. This chapter will give a brief description of the group before discussing the group's market-orientation, "segmentation, targeting, and position" (STP), internal marketing, public diplomacy, and nation branding strategies and activities.

Keywords Zionism • Anti-semitism • Sales-orientation • Segments • Psychological positioning • Base strategy • Public diplomacy

Overview

AIJAC is a think tank and advocacy group dedicated to representing the Australian Jewish community to the government, media, and other civil society actors. It was formed in 1997 through the merger of two earlier

© The Author(s), under exclusive license to Springer Nature Switzerland AG 2022
A. Lim, *Political Marketing and Public Diplomacy by Pro-Israel and Pro-Palestinian Advocacy Groups*, Palgrave Studies in Political Marketing and Management,
https://doi.org/10.1007/978-3-031-15332-7_4

Jewish organisations: Australia-Israel Publications (AIP) and the think tank Australian Institute of Jewish Affairs (AIJA). While it devotes much of its informational output and advocacy work to Israel and the Middle East, AIJAC also deals with other issues of concern to the Australian Jewish community such as Islamism, terrorism, racism (including anti-Semitism), religious intolerance, war crimes justice, Holocaust denial, multiculturalism, and democracy. Its activities have included sponsoring guest speaking engagements, educational missions to Israel and the West Bank, publishing a monthly magazine called *Australia/Israel Review* (*AIR*), and networking with other like-minded civil society groups and activists in Australia and the Jewish diaspora (Gawenda, 2020; Reich, 2004).

Marketing Orientation

AIJAC has pursued sales-based orientation by producing content that appeals to its Australian-Jewish and pro-Israel audience. Drawing upon Lees-Marshment's (2004) "Market/Sales/Product-Oriented" charity framework, AIJAC can be classified as a sales-oriented advocacy group that follows the five stages of a sales-oriented group, which are outlined in Table 4.1:

Analysis

In terms of marketing orientation, AIJAC has followed the five-stage process associated with sales-oriented advocacy groups. First, AIJAC has promoted its product (defending Israel, Australian-Jewish interests, combating anti-Semitism and racism). Second, AIJAC conducted market intelligence by seeking to co-opt sympathetic political elites, media, and civil society actors through its communications output and advocacy work particularly its guest speaker programme and Ramban information trips. Third, AIJAC has disseminated its messages and arguments on accessible, modern communications technologies such as its website, *AIR* magazine, social media platforms, and email newsletters to maximise its outreach. Fourth, AIJAC has used its advocacy activities including short-term campaigning to influence political, media and public opinion on Israel-Palestine. Finally, AIJAC has used its communications output to promote its work and achievements including its official role in facilitating Netanyahu's 2017 state visit and media management work.

Table 4.1 AIJAC analysed using Lees-Marshment's sales-oriented framework

Stages	Definitions	Examples
Product design	Design a wide range of behaviour in accordance to what they think is right or works best.	Advocating on issues of interest to the Australian Jewish community including Israel, anti-Semitism, Islamism, terrorism, racism and religious intolerance, war crimes justice, and Holocaust denial. Commitment to democracy, human rights, free speech, and multiculturalism in Australia and combating forms of extremism and fundamentalism (ACNC, 2019; Reich, 2004).
Market intelligence	Identify the groups and segments of the public most likely to support it, using market segmentation to target them, and discuss how best to influence and persuade them.	Segmenting influential political, media, and civil society actors into sympathetic and hostile elements based on how they align with AIJAC's goals and agenda. It has targeted them through its communications media, guest speaker programme, and its Ramban Israel Fellowship missions. For example, sympathetic segments can include Labor and Coalition politicians while hostile elements would include the Greens and One Nation (Gawenda, 2020; Han & Rane, 2013; Loewenstein, 2006; Reich, 2004).
Communication	Proactive, entertaining communication designed to attract attention, influence the public and civil society, raise income from potential supporters; using a wide range of marketing techniques such as pamphlets, posters, websites, Facebook, and Twitter.	Using its monthly magazine, the *Australia/Israel Review* (*AIR*), website (https://aijac.org.au), email newsletter, and Facebook (https://www.facebook.com/aijac.au), Twitter (https://twitter.com/AIJAC_Update), and YouTube (https://www.youtube.com/user/AIJACvideo) social media accounts to disseminate information.

(*continued*)

Table 4.1 (continued)

Stages	Definitions	Examples
Campaign	Short-term, one-off appeals; for example, media campaigns and influencing policy-makers and other actors	Engaging in advocacy activities such as lobbying, its guest speaker programme, and the Ramban information trips (Gawenda, 2020; Reich, 2004). Covering Israel-related current affairs events such as the 2012 and 2014 Gaza Wars, Prime Minister Netanyahu's state visit to Australia in February 2017, the Gaza March of Return, and the 2018 Nation State law (AIJAC, 2017b; Falkenstein, 2014; Fleischer, 2012; Fleischer, 2018; Rubenstein, 2018c).
Delivery	Deliver what it thinks is best, promoting it in the most positive way possible.	Using its print and online output to publicise its advocacy activities and achievements including hosting Netanyahu's state visit to Australia, winning a media complaint against the public broadcaster Special Broadcasting Service's (SBS') coverage of the 2018 Gaza March of Return, and challenging journalist Lyons' alleged anti-Israel bias (AIJAC, 2017b, 2018h; Fleischer, 2017).

SEGMENTATION, TARGETING, AND POSITIONING (STP)

Segmentation

AIJAC appears to follow all three stages of Bartle and Griffiths' (2002) "segmentation, targeting, and positioning" (STP) process. Though AIJAC was not forthcoming about their segmentation practices, this research found circumstantial evidence that AIJAC did conduct some degree of segmentation by cooperating with "friendly" political and civil society actors which shared its pro-Israel goals and worldview while opposing "hostile" political, media, and civil society actors that did not share these goals and worldview. "Friendly" political segments have included senior leaders and policy-makers from Australia's two major political parties: the Liberal-National Coalition and the Australian Labor Party (AIJAC, 2015f, 2016b; The Face-Off, 2013). Reflecting its insider relationship with the two major parties, AIJAC's national board of directors regularly meets with senior Coalition and Labor leaders to consult on issues concerning Israel and the Australian Jewish community. Besides the-then Prime Minister Malcolm Turnbull and Minister for Foreign Affairs Julie Bishop, AIJAC has also met with senior Labor figures including Leader of the Opposition Bill Shorten, Shadow Foreign Minister Tania Plibersek, and Jewish Members of Parliament (MPs) Mark Dreyfus and Michael Danby to maintain bipartisan support for Israel (AIJAC, 2015d, 2016b). During the 2013 Australian federal election, AIJAC submitted questions regarding Israel, Iran and the Boycott, Divestment, and Sanctions (BDS) movement to both the Liberal and Labor party leaders ("The Face-Off,", 2013; Mittelman, 2013). These interactions show that AIJAC has placed great importance in winning over Australian political elites and policy-makers who are in a position to influence Australian foreign policy towards Israel as well as other issues of interest to the Australian Jewish community such as Islamism, terrorism, racism (including anti-Semitism), and multiculturalism.

Other "friendly" segments have included other Jewish and Zionist civil society groups, media, and figures within Australia and the global Jewish diaspora:

- Within Australia, AIJAC has cooperated with other Jewish and Zionist organisations including the Australian Voices for Israel, Sydney's Central Synagogue, the United Israel Appeal (UIA), Zionist Council of New South Wales, and the Executive Council of Australian Jewry (ECAJ) by co-hosting guest speaking functions and issuing joint statements on issues affecting Australian Jews (AIJAC, 2014a, 2015a, 2016j, 2018d).
- AIJAC also appears to have a cordial relationship with local Jewish media such as the *Australian Jewish News* (AJN) and J-Wire. AJN has covered AIJAC's advocacy work including its meetings with senior Australian policy-makers, a successful AIJAC complaint against the Australian Broadcasting Corporation (ABC), and efforts to lobby the Australian Government on a "biased" UNESCO (United Nations Educational, Scientific and Cultural Organization) resolution and foreign aid policies (AIJAC, 2016b, 2016d, 2016). Similarly, J-Wire has covered AIJAC's activities including its engagement with senior Labour politicians, Ramban missions for Victorian state MPs and Indonesian Muslim civil society leaders and educators, AIJAC's opposition to the far-right One Nation party, and an AIJAC-sponsored

luncheon in Sydney for attendees of the 2016 Beersheba Dialogue (AIJAC, 2015f, 2016e, 2016f, 2016h, 2017a). In return, AIJAC (2017j, December 14; 2018a, January 10) has shared J-Wire stories including a 2017 motion by the National Council of Students condemning anti-Semitism and the murder of Israeli medic Razie Shevah.
- AIJAC has also worked with the Jewish historian and social scientist Ran Porat, a researcher at Monash University's Australian Centre for Jewish Civilisation. As a guest columnist for *AIR* magazine, Porat (2018a, 2018b) has written articles covering anti-Semitism within the Australian Arab ethnic media and Muslim community.
- On a global level, AIJAC maintains a formal partnership with the American Jewish Committee (AJC), a major Jewish American advocacy group. The two organisations collaborate to promote a greater understanding of the issues and challenges facing world Jewry in the Asia-Pacific region (AIJAC, n.d.; Reich, 2004).

These interactions show that AIJAC has cultivated relationships with various Jewish and Zionist civil society groups, media, and figures in both Australia and abroad. These "friendly" segments work with AIJAC since they share its goals in advancing the interests and aspirations of Israel and the global Jewish diaspora including Australia. Thus, they work together to organise events and gatherings, publicise each other's activities, and share their resources, knowledge, and expertise. Cooperation with like-minded groups and individuals helps to connect AIJAC to both the wider Australian Jewish community and the global Jewish diaspora.

In addition to these "friendly" segments, the author identified several segments which had a "hostile" relationship with AIJAC. These various political, media, and civil society actors did not share AIJAC's goals and interests especially on Israel-related issues. Seven of these "hostile" segments are listed below:

- The **Australian Greens** is a left-wing political party that advocates on environmental and social justice issues. AIJAC opposes the Greens' perceived pro-Palestinian policies and view of Israel as a "racist, Apartheid state" (A. Shapiro, 2016c).
- The **Australian Jewish Democratic Society** (AJDS) is a progressive Jewish organisation that has advocated on Palestinian human rights issues and criticised Israeli policies and actions towards the Palestinians (Mendes, 2016). AIJAC's Executive Director Colin Rubenstein has

claimed that AJDS is a "fringe group" that does not represent the views of Australian Jewish community (Reich, 2004, p. 202).
- **Bob Carr** is a retired Labor politician who once served as the Premier of New South Wales and Foreign Minister in the Gillard Government. AIJAC's conflict with Carr dates back to the Palestinian Liberation Organisation (PLO) official Dr Hanan Ashrawi's 2003 Sydney Peace Prize (Levey & Mendes, 2004; Loewenstein, 2006). AIJAC has responded to Carr's criticisms of Israeli settlements (AIJAC, 2012a; Narunsky, 2017), "Israel lobby" allegations (Mittelman, 2015a), and Israel's rightward political shift (Debinski & Shapiro, 2014). They have also criticised his association with pro-Palestinian advocates including the Australian Friends of Palestine Association and the Al Quds Community Centre (Jones, 2018).
- **Jake Lynch** is a former journalist turned academic who headed the University of Sydney's former Centre for Peace and Conflict Studies (CPCS), which has drawn AIJAC's criticism for endorsing the BDS campaign by boycotting Israeli academics and institutions (Hyams, 2011). AIJAC has criticised Lynch's pro-Palestinian activism including hosting Palestinian activist Sameh Habeeb and disrupting British pro-Israel advocate Colonel Richard Kemp's talk at Sydney University (Falkenstein, 2015; Meyerowitz-Katz, 2012c).
- **John Lyons** was *The Australian* newspaper's former Middle East correspondent and currently works for the ABC. AIJAC has criticised his coverage on the eviction of Palestinian families, settlement expansion, the Israeli military's detention of Palestinian minors, and his controversial *Stone Cold Justice* documentary on ABC's Four Corners (Fleischer, 2017). In response, Lyons (2017) has criticised AIJAC in his memoir *Balcony over Jerusalem,* alleging that AIJAC harassed journalists who it deemed "anti-Israel," prompting AIJAC to defend their media management activities (A. Shapiro, 2017c).
- **Sophie McNeill** was the ABC's former Middle East correspondent. AIJAC objected to the ABC's decision to hire McNeill as their Middle East correspondent, alleging that her alleged pro-Palestinian sympathies and ties to Palestinian civil society groups compromised her objectivity (A. Shapiro, 2015). AIJAC has criticised her coverage of the Gaza Blockade, the 2014 Gaza War, and the Israeli military's demolition of Palestinian homes, alleging that they cast Israel in a negative light and legitimised Palestinian violence (A. Shapiro, 2016a, 2016b; Lee, 2015a, 2015b, 2015c, 2016a).

- **Pauline Hanson's One Nation party** is a far-right minor party known for its anti-immigration and anti-Muslim positions. AIJAC rejects their exclusivist White supremacist agenda as incongruent with its vision of a pluralistic, multicultural, and tolerant Australia (Falkenstein & Narunsky, 2016). AIJAC has historically opposed far-right extremism in Australia and objected to visits by far-right activists including the Holocaust denier David Irving, the Nation of Islam's leader Louis Farrakhan, and the Lyndon LaRouche movement. In 1998, AIJAC controversially published One Nation's secret membership list (Reich, 2004).

These findings suggest that AIJAC has identified both "friendly" and "hostile" segments based on how their ideologies and actions align with AIJAC's goals and worldview. Besides seeking to maintain bipartisan political support for Israel in Australia, AIJAC seeks to combat various political, media, and civil society figures and groups whom it considers hostile to Israel and Australian Jewish interests. Despite their usefulness, they are largely speculative since they were based on the author's analysis of AIJAC's public statements and activities rather than their stated segmentation policies; which the organisation has been unwilling to disclose. Future research can hopefully shed light on AIJAC's segmentation policies.

Targeting

AIJAC (n.d.; Gawenda, 2020; Han & Rane, 2013; Loewenstein, 2006; Reich, 2004) has targeted sympathetic political, media, and civil society leaders, as well as interested members of the public through a range of relational activities and communicational output including the following:

- A "Visitor programme," which brings international speakers to Australia and New Zealand.
- The "Ramban Israel Fellowship" programme, which brings journalists, politicians, political advisers, senior public servants, student leaders, and other civil society leaders on informational trips to Israel.
- AIJAC Forum was an internship programme recruiting young professionals into AIJAC's activities around Canberra and Australia. At the time of publication, the programme appears to have been discontinued.

- Publishing a monthly magazine called *Australia/Israel Review*, which covers developments in the Middle East affecting Israel and issues of interest to the Australian Jewish community. The magazine is available in both print and digital editions with selected articles published on AIJAC's website. Besides its magazine, AIJAC analysts and staff members have also engaged with the media through op-ed columns, letters, and interviews, reflecting the organisation's interest in managing Australian media coverage and commentary on Israel-Palestine issues.
- AIJAC also publishes a current affairs blog on its website called "Fresh AIR" which features its latest research and commentary. AIJAC also produces a free email newsletter called "Update on AIJAC." In addition, AIJAC also maintains accounts on several social media platforms including Facebook, Twitter, and YouTube.

AIJAC uses these relational activities and communications output to influence Australian political, media, and public opinion towards Israel in a favourable direction. Besides promoting pro-Israel narratives and combating so-called anti-Israel propaganda and activism, they also seek to convince key Australian stakeholders and institutions to adopt policies and practices that benefit Israeli and Jewish communal interests and aspirations. In short, AIJAC has conducted informal public diplomacy on behalf of Israel, a topic discussed in the final section.

Positioning

Third, AIJAC conducted "psychological positioning" to manage Israel's public image in Australia. Whereas "real positioning" seeks to alter the product to cater for the market, psychological positioning focuses on altering perceptions of their product (Bartle & Griffiths, 2002). In practice, the organisation has sought to manage Israel's international image in Australia by combating negative coverage and perceptions while highlighting positive stories about Israel. Based on a content analysis of AIJAC's webpages, social media, and audio-visual content, the groups' information output can be categorised into seven major themes and narratives:

- **Israel has always acted in self-defence against genuine security threats**. AIJAC has framing Israeli military actions during the 2010

Mavi Marmara raid, the 2012 and 2014 Gaza Wars, and the 2018 Gaza March of Return as legitimate and proportionate responses to Palestinian terrorism and violence (AIJAC, 2010; AIJAC, 2014c, 2018e; Fleischer, 2012). This coverage is intended to address the asymmetry in power between Israel and the Palestinians by framing Israel as a righteous combatant that acts in self-defence and abides by international law governing warfare.

- **Israel wanting peace with the Palestinians and the wider Arab-Muslim world.** As evidence, AIJAC has cited Israel's stated commitment to a two-state solution alongside peace initiatives such as the Gilad Shalit prisoner exchange, the repatriation of deceased Palestinian prisoners, and efforts to expand diplomatic relations with the United Arab Emirates (AIJAC, 2015a; AIJAC, 2015g; Mittelman, 2012; Rubenstein, 2011).
- **Israel is a genuine democracy that protects the rights of ethnic and religious minorities.** In terms of ethnic minorities, AIJAC has highlighted positive stories about Israeli programmes to aid Palestinian children such as Project Rozana, Israeli Arabs studying at Israeli universities, and collaboration between Arab and Jewish medical professionals (AIJAC, 2014d, 2015c, 2017c; Meyerowitz-Katz, 2012b). In terms of religious freedom, AIJAC has highlighted stories about Israel protecting the rights of Christian citizens, issuing permits to allow Palestinian Christians to celebrate Christmas in Jerusalem, and Israel appointing its first female Sharia court judge Hana Khatib (AIJAC, 2014b, 2012c, 2017d). These stories are intended to combat the negative image of Israel as an "Apartheid" state that privileges its Jewish citizens over non-Jews.
- **Israel is a prosperous, innovative country and good international citizen.** In support of Israeli public diplomacy and nation branding, AIJAC has highlighted stories about Israeli economic prosperity, water and agricultural technologies, disaster management policies, the information technology industry, and solar energy (Asa-El, 2018; A. Shapiro, 2012; Rubenstein, 2016a; "Yosef Abramowitz on Israel's green energy outreach, human rights and environmental activism," 2018). To promote the image of Israel as a good international citizen, AIJAC has also highlighted Israel's disaster relief efforts during the Syrian Civil War, the 2018 Tham Luang cave rescue, and the 2018 Volcán de Fuego eruption in Guatemala (A. Shapiro, 2013; AIJAC, 2015f, 2018g). These stories are used to

counter the negative imagery about Israel by highlighting Israel's positive contributions to the international community.
- **The Palestinians have rejected peace with Israel and sought to undermine Israel through violence, terrorism, and political intransigence**. AIJAC has claimed that the Palestinian Authority has rejected Israel's peace offers and is using the United Nations as an instrument to exert pressure on Israel (Fleischer, 2013; Rubenstein, 2017a). AIJAC has also published stories about the Palestinian Authority and Hamas misappropriate humanitarian aid money for terrorism purposes including the "Pay to Slay" programme (Burack, 2018; Rubenstein, 2016b), anti-Israel incitement and indoctrination (AIJAC, 2016e, 2018a), and President Mahmoud Abbas rejecting Israel's historical claims to the Holy Land (AIJAC, 2017i). Hamas, which governs the Gaza Strip, is presented as an anti-Semitic terror organisation seeking to destroy Israel. AIJAC has published stories about Hamas's anti-Israel hostility (A. Shapiro, 2017a), indoctrinating Palestinian youths into "terrorist fighters" (Avi-Guy, 2013), using human shields (AIJAC, 2012b), firing incendiary kites and rockets into Israel (AIJAC, 2018c, 2018g), and blaming Hamas for instigating the 2012 and 2014 Gaza Wars and the 2018 March of Return (Asa-El, 2012, 2014; Rubenstein, 2018d). In short, AIJAC advances the Israeli narrative that the Palestinians are the aggressors while justifying Israeli policies and actions against them.
- **Anti-Semitism is a major threat to Jewish existence and self-determination**. Besides combating Holocaust denial and far-right anti-Semitism, AIJAC has also covered Arab-Muslim anti-Semitism and the BDS movement. AIJAC has produced content highlighting anti-Semitic and anti-Israel sentiment within the Australian Muslim community, media, and religious material and attributing Jihadi terror attacks such as the Hypercacher kosher supermarket siege and the 2015 Charlie Hebdo attack to Muslim anti-Semitism (Ahmed, 2016; AIJAC, 2015d, 2015e; Porat, 2018a). AIJAC opposes the BDS Movement, regarding it as an anti-Israel hate movement masquerading as a human rights movement. Besides monitoring local BDS campaigns such as the Max Brenner boycott campaign and the Marrickville Council's 2010 Israel divestment policy (Meyerowitz-Katz, 2011), the group has also published content highlighting the alleged anti-Semitic nature of the movement such as the intimidation of Jewish university students and the boycott action against the DC

superhero film *Wonder Woman* due to the lead actress Gal Gadot's Israeli citizenship and Jewish ethnicity (AIJAC, 2016a; Beroff, 2017). In short, AIJAC's coverage of Arab-Muslim anti-Semitism and the BDS Movement seeks to attribute their hostility towards Israel to a visceral hatred for Jews rather than opposition to Israeli policies and actions towards the Palestinians.

- **Zionism is a Jewish self-determination movement that seeks to restore Jews to their ancestral homeland of Israel.** While AIJAC (n.d.) does not explicitly describe itself as a Zionist organisation, it supports most Zionist ideas and goals such as the centrality of Israel to Jewish identity and security and combating the various manifestations of anti-Semitism. AIJAC regards Jerusalem as the indivisible capital of Israel, a mainstream Israeli and Zionist position (Mittelman, 2015b). It has also defended controversial Israeli policies such as Israeli settlements and the Nation State Law, citing Zionist arguments about ethnic groups being entitled to national homelands (Fleischer, 2016; Rubenstein, 2018c). For AIJAC, Zionism represents the Jewish expression of nationhood and self-determination.

Based on these seven key arguments and narratives, AIJAC's positioning strategies consist of defending Israeli military actions against the Palestinians, marketing the positive aspects of Israel, shifting blame for the Arab-Israeli conflict onto the Palestinian side, framing opposition towards Israel as a form of anti-Semitism, and defending the legitimacy of Zionism. The group seeks to combat growing public perceptions of Israel as the "Goliath" oppressing the Palestinians and Zionism as a racist "settler-colonial ideology." AIJAC also tries to link popular causes such as combating racism and anti-Semitism to fighting groups and movements which it deems anti-Israel such as the BDS movement. In short, AIJAC seeks to convince their Australian audience that Israel is right and the Palestinians are wrong. AIJAC's pro-Israel messages and arguments show that the group sees itself as working with the Israeli Government and sympathetic pro-Israel groups and activists to defend Israel's international image and preserve the connection between Israel and the global Jewish diaspora.

Analysis

AIJAC has fulfilled all three stages of the STP process. First, it has segmented political, media, and civil society elites in Australia and its "near abroad" into friendly and hostile segments. These were based on the researcher's observations of AIJAC's communications output and relational activities as opposed to insider knowledge. Second, AIJAC has targeted sympathetic elites who can influence policies and public opinion towards Israel and the Jewish Diaspora by allocating resources to reaching them via its communications and advocacy activities, particularly its *AIR* magazine, website, email newsletters, guest speaker programme, and Ramban information trips. Third, AIJAC conducted psychological positioning by publishing content defending Israel's actions, promoting favourable aspects of Israel and Zionism, shifting blame onto the Palestinian side, and framing opposition to Israel as being motivated by anti-Semitism.

Internal Marketing

Drawing upon several primary and secondary sources, this research found that the organisation pursues a "base strategy." Pettitt (2015) defines a base strategy as one that involves mobilising activists by pushing a product that appeals to the group's most committed supporters. According to AIJAC (n.d.) and ACNC (2019), the organisation is committed to the following goals and values:

- Conveying the interests of the Australian Jewish community to government, media, and community organisations;
- Combating anti-Israel bias and "misinformation" in the media and wider public debate;
- Promoting tolerance and multiculturalism;
- Combating racism, anti-Semitism, extremism, and fundamentalism; and
- Educating the Australian public and elites about Israel and other issues of interest to Australian Jewry.

These primary documents show that AIJAC has a clearly defined set of goals and values which its members and supporters are expected to follow. As a think tank and lobbying outfit, its staff members are expected to engage in research and advocacy work that advances these goals.

These primary sources were corroborated by observations from the secondary literature:

- According to Reich (2004) and Gawenda (2020), AIJAC's Executive Director Colin Rubenstein envisioned AIJAC as a professional lobbying organisation and think tank along the lines of the American Israel Public Affairs Committee (AIPAC) and the American Jewish Committee that would produce information, research, and lobby on issues of importance to Australian Jewry.
- According to Han and Rane (2013), AIJAC has advocated on issues of concern to Australian Jewry including racism, anti-Semitism, terrorism, maintaining Jewish identity, autonomy and communal survival, anti-Zionism, Israeli sovereignty and security, and anti-Israel "bias" in the media and academia. They have also promoted the Australian Jewish community's solidarity and commitment to Israel through fundraising, Aliyah (emigration to Israel), and cultural and religious identification with Israel.
- According to Gawenda (2020), Rubenstein ran AIJAC as a private advocacy organisation that operated independently of the ECAJ, the major Jewish representative organisation in Australia. This research found that Rubenstein has largely succeeded in these goals due to AIJAC's substantial communications output, research, and extensive advocacy works.

Based on these primary and secondary sources, AIJAC pursues a base strategy, since its ideological commitment to advancing Israel, Zionism, and Jewish communal interests drives its activities and attracts like-minded personnel and supporters. As a professional lobbying body, AIJAC does not have mass membership but seeks to recruit skilled personnel with a background in media, research, and who are able to network with influential political, media, civil society, and business elites.

Analysis

In terms of internal marketing, the research showed that AIJAC pursues a base strategy that appeals to issues of concern to Australian Jewry including Israel, racism, anti-Semitism, promoting democracy and multiculturalism, and combating extremism and fundamentalism. AIJAC also sees itself and operates as a lobbying organisation and think tank devoted to raising these issues to Australian society through its communications output and advocacy work. AIJAC seeks to recruit members who share its aims and goals and who are thus motivated by a sense of loyalty and purpose towards advancing these goals.

Public Diplomacy and Nation Branding

AIJAC has supported Israeli public diplomacy and nation branding by networking with Israeli policy-makers and officials, producing pro-Israel informational output, and sponsoring guest speakers through its Visitor programme and informational trips to Israel through its "Ramban Israel Fellowship." These communicational output and relational activities seek to manage Israel's international image in Australia and promote Israel's culture, heritage, and national identity.

First, AIJAC has cultivated relations and networked with senior Israeli policy-makers and officials while leveraging on its high-level access to Australian political elites:

- In November 2016, its National Chairman Mark Leibler met with Israeli Prime Minister Benjamin Netanyahu; demonstrating the organisation's ability to gain high-level access to the Israeli Government (AIJAC, 2016i).
- On February 22, 2017, Leibler officiated over two public events during Netanyahu's state visit to Australia. At the request of Prime Minister Malcolm Turnbull's office, Leibler hosted a luncheon between Netanyahu and several Australian business leaders focusing on bilateral trade and economic cooperation. Later that evening, Leibler hosted Netanyahu and Turnbull during a Jewish community function at Sydney's Central Synagogue. To generate favourable publicity, several senior AIJAC staff members produced newspaper op-eds and took part in interviews with several Australian, Israel, and New Zealand media outlets (AIJAC, 2017b).
- To promote Australian-Israeli defence cooperation, AIJAC has worked with the Australian Strategic Policy Institute (ASPI) and the Begin-Sadat (BESA) Center for Strategic Studies at Bar Ilan University to host the Beersheba Dialogue, an annual meeting of Israeli and Australian strategic analysts and defence experts. Following the 2016 Beersheba Dialogue, AIJAC (2016h) hosted a luncheon and public talk at Sydney's Central Synagogue featuring Israeli and Australian defence officials. During the third Beersheba Dialogue in November 2017, Turnbull signed a Memorandum of Understanding on defence industry cooperation (AIJAC, 2017h).

AIJAC's access to heads of governments and involvement in official functions reflects its "insider" relationships with both the Australian and Israeli governments, who recognise it as a legitimate representative of the Australian Jewish community. These activities also show that AIJAC has sought to deepen Australian-Israeli bilateral relations on various fronts including the interpersonal, economic, civil society, and defence dimensions.

Second, AIJAC has used its print, online, and audio-visual informational output to promote Israeli public diplomacy and nation branding by managing Israel's media image and highlighting the positive aspects of Australian-Israeli bilateral relations:

- In terms of media management, AIJAC has published pro-Israel op-ed columns and letters in several major Australian newspapers and media platforms including *The Age, The Australian,* the ABC, the *Australian Financial Review, Canberra Times, Daily Telegraph, Herald Sun,* and the *Sydney Morning Herald* (Hyams, 2014; Meyerowitz-Katz, 2012a; Mittelman, 2018; Ostrovsky, 2011; Rubenstein, 2014, 2017a, 2017b, 2018b). In addition, AIJAC has participated in media interviews and news reports with major Australian news broadcasters including the ABC, Sky News Australia, and SBS (ABC News24, 2017; SBS World News, 2018; Sky News AM Agenda, 2018).
- In terms of political relations, AIJAC has highlighted Israeli Prime Minister Netanyahu's 2017 state visit to Australia and both federal and state governments' expressions of support for Israel (S. Levin, 2017; AIJAC, 2018f; Lerman, 2017).
- In terms of historical ties, A. Shapiro (2017d) highlighted the centenary of the Battle of Beersheba in October 2017, emphasising the Australia and New Zealand Army Corps (ANZAC) Mounted Division's contributions to the British victory in the Palestine campaign of the First World War, which he argued paved the way for the Balfour Declaration and the subsequent establishment of Israel.
- In terms of economic relations, AIJAC has highlighted Woodside Petroleum's 2012 investment in Israel's Leviathan natural gas field, cooperation between local governments, start-up companies, and the agricultural sector in Australia and Israel (AIJAC, 2012d, 2016c, 2017g; Rubenstein, 2016a).

To support Israeli public diplomacy and nation branding, AIJAC has submitted pro-Israel op-ed columns and letters to major Australian media outlets while also taking part in media interviews and news reports. In addition, AIJAC has published content highlighting the various political, historical, and economic dimensions of the Australian-Israel bilateral relationship. Taken together, AIJAC seeks to convince its audience that Australia and Israel are friendly allies with shared values and interests.

Third, AIJAC has used its "Visitor programme" and Ramban Israel Fellowship to promote Israeli public diplomacy and nation branding on a relational level. As part of its Visitor programme, AIJAC has brought international guest speakers to speak at private and public functions across Australia and New Zealand in cooperation with Jewish community organisations and synagogues. Notable guest speakers have included:

- Israeli political figures including former Israeli Labor parliamentarian and Dr Einat Wilf, Likud parliamentarian and government minister Tzachi Hanegbi, former Israeli National Security Council (NSC) member Dr Eran Lerman, and former Israel Defense Forces (IDF) spokesperson Lt Colonel Peter Lerner. These guest speakers covered a range of topics including the BDS movement, anti-Zionism, and Israeli settlements (AIJAC, 2016b, 2018d; Mittelman, 2015c, November 4; A. Shapiro, 2017b).
- Israeli civil society and media representatives including Israeli-Arab Channel 2 broadcaster Lucy Aharish and green solar entrepreneur Yosef Abramowitz. Aharish spoke about Israeli Arab lives and integration while Abramowitz talked about Israel's solar industry (Mittelman, 2016; "Yosef Abramowitz on Israel's green energy outreach, human rights and environmental activism," 2018).
- Dissident Palestinian activist Bassem Eid's talk in August 2015 about the two-state solution, Palestinian Authority, BDS movement, and peace through economic development. Eid is the founder of the Palestinian Human Rights Monitoring Group and supports normalisation with Israel ("Bassem Eid on prospects for a Palestinian state," 2015).
- Middle East Forum (MEF) President Daniel Pipes' Melbourne 2018 public lecture on the Middle East (AIJAC, 2018b). Pipes is a neo-conservative American intellectual who founded MEF, a conservative pro-Israel think tank focusing on the Middle East and Islamism.

In response to criticism of Pipes' 2018 Australian tour, Rubenstein (2018a) disputed allegations of Islamophobia against him.

Despite their varied backgrounds and trades, these guest speakers share AIJAC's worldview about Israel's centrality to Jewish society and culture. Besides fostering Australian Jewish diaspora connections with Israel and abroad, these talks help to promote a positive image of an inclusive and resilient Israel. For example, the presence of Israeli-Arab broadcaster Aharish helps combat the narrative of Israel being a racist, Apartheid state while hosting dissident Palestinian voices like Eid helps to reinforce criticism of the BDS movement as an anti-Semitic hate movement. Hosting Abramowitz highlights Israel's green energy industry and efforts to combat climate change and pollution.

AIJAC has used its Ramban Israel Fellowship programme to bring political, media, and civil society leaders including journalists, student leaders, trade unionists, and religious leaders on informational trips to Israel and the Palestinian Territories. The Ramban programme was started by Sydney businessman Brian Sherman in late 2003 to "lift the veil" on Israel for opinion-makers in response to the Second Intifada (AIJAC, n.d.; Loewenstein, 2006; Reich, 2004). According to Jones (2016), the Ramban programme exposes people in Australia and the Asia-Pacific to a wide range of viewpoints, educates them about Israeli geography, history, cultural diversity, and society, and enables them to meet with Israeli and Palestinian leaders, experts, and activists from across the spectrum. According to Gawenda (2020), Ramban is supported by private donations from several wealthy Australian Jewish families. By 2020, about 500 individuals including journalists, commentators, senior public servants, and academics had participated in the Ramban programme. Notable Ramban participants have included:

- **Politicians**: Notable Liberal participants have included Bradfield MP Paul Fletcher, Tasmanian Senator David Bushby, Paterson MP Bob Baldwin, South Australian Senator David Fawcett, Brisbane MP Teresa Gambaro, Cowan MP Luke Simpkins, Liberal National MP Mal Brough, Senator Sean C. Edwards, South Australian MP Corey Wingard, and Prime Minister Scott Morrison (Narunsky, 2012; AIJAC, 2015b; "Corey Wingard MP (South Australia)—Impressions of Israel," 2017; Gawenda, 2020). Notable Labor participants have

included the Victorian Parliamentary Secretary to the Premier Colin Brooks, Deputy Speaker Don Nardella, Government Whip Ros Spence, and Victorian State Parliament MPs Lizzie Blandthorn, Josh Bull, Paul Edbrooke, Nick Staikos, Vicki Ward, Gabrielle Williams, and veteran MP Marsha Thomson (AIJAC, 2016d). Other participants have included MP Julian Hill, Labor senior advisers Thomas Mooney and Sandy Kay-Oswald, Senators Kristina Keneally and Anthony Chisholm, former Prime Minister Julia Gillard, and former Labor leader Bill Shorten (AIJAC, 2017e, 2018f; Gawenda, 2020).
- **Journalists**: *Herald & Weekly Times* editor-in-chief Peter Blunden and journalist John Ferguson, the *Australian Financial Review*'s Ben Potter and Robert Bolton, *The Age*'s chief editorial writer Jon Watson, the *Courier Mail*'s Dennis Atkins, SBS journalist Sally Watson, the *Sydney Morning Herald* journalist Louise Dodson, and Channel Ten journalist John Hill (Loewenstein, 2006).
- **Indonesian Muslim leaders and educators**: In January 2017, AIJAC's Director of International & Community Affairs Jeremy Jones took these Muslim civil society leaders on a tour of Israel and the Palestinian Territories, focusing on Muslim-Jewish interfaith dialogue. Participants visited Bethlehem, Ramallah, the "planned city" of Rawabi, Al Aqsa Mosque, Church of the Holy Sepulchre, Gaza's border, and the Golan Heights (AIJAC, 2017a). Reflects AIJAC's efforts to promote understanding and reconciliation between Muslims and Jews.
- **Trade unionists**: Diana Asmar of Health Services Union Victoria and Glen Chatterton of the Plumbers Union Service Trade Queensland took part in a Ramban mission in 2017, which focused on fostering bilateral trade union ties, water technology transfer, and visiting Israeli Arab doctors at hospitals (AIJAC, 2017f).

AIJAC's Ramban Fellowships show that it has sponsored politically oriented trips to Israel and the Palestinian Territories in order to promote support for Israel and cultivate relations with influential political, media, religious, and trade union figures. The inclusion of Indonesian Muslim leaders and educators shows that AIJAC's operations are not limited to Australia and that the organisation is interested in promoting interfaith dialogue between Jews and Muslims to promote peace.

Analysis

AIJAC has engaged in pro-Israel public diplomacy and nation branding through various communicational and relational activities. First, AIJAC has successfully cultivated relations with senior Israeli policy-makers and officials while leveraging on its high-level access to Australian political elites. Reflecting its high-level access to both Israeli and Australian government figures and institutions, AIJAC has helped host official state visits and meetings between heads of government and policy-makers in both countries. Second, AIJAC has published various online, print, and audio-visual communications output highlighting the positive aspects of Australian-Israel bilateral relations. In addition, AIJAC has sought to manage Israel's media image by producing op-ed content in major Australian news outlets and participating in media interviews and reports. These media contacts sought to counter negative imagery and criticism of Israel in response to crises and conflicts.

Third, AIJAC has used its Visitor and Ramban information trip programmes to promote support for Israel to sympathetic members of the Australian public, political elites, media, and civil society leaders. The Visitor programme provides a platform for various Israeli and pro-Israel figures to communicate with Australian and New Zealand audiences. Meanwhile, Ramban information trips seek to promote Israel's culture, heritage, and identity while combating negative perceptions of Israel through contact with Israelis and Palestinians and educating them about Israel's geography, history, culture, and society.

Conclusion

This chapter analysed the communications and advocacy activities of the Australia/Israel & Jewish Affairs Council against the researcher's political marketing and public diplomacy framework. AIJAC met most of the criteria of this framework. In terms of market-orientation, AIJAC has followed the five stages of a sales-oriented charity. First, AIJAC's product consists of advocating on Israel and other issues of interest to Australian Jews. Second, AIJAC has conducted some market intelligence by identifying influential Australian political, media, and civil society elites who can influence official policies and public opinion towards Israel-Palestine. Third, AIJAC has used its online, print, and audio-visual output to communicate its messages and arguments. Fourth, AIJAC has conducted campaigning through targeted lobbying campaigns and covering Israel-related issues in response to newsworthy events. Finally, AIJAC has used its communications output to report successful political and media advocacy campaigns.

Second, AIJAC has followed all three stages of the "segmentation, targeting, and positioning" (STP) process. First, AIJAC's communications output and various secondary sources showed that AIJAC segmented its market into "friendly" segments it could work with and "hostile" segments that it needed to oppose. Second, AIJAC has targeted friendly segments through its communications output, guest speaking, and information trip programmes. Third, AIJAC conducted psychological positioning by framing Israel's military actions as self-defence, raising awareness about Israel's positive attributes, shifting blame onto the Palestinians, highlighting the dangers of anti-Semitism and anti-Zionism, and defending the legitimacy of Zionism.

Third, AIJAC has used a base strategy to encourage its members to carry out communications and relational activities by appealing to their commitment to Israel, Zionism, and advancing Jewish communal interests. Pettitt's base strategy was the most relevant internal marketing model since it supported the research findings that the AIJAC designed its product around the needs and expectations of its pro-Israel internal stakeholders. As part of its base strategy, the IINZ informed supporters about its efforts to represent the concerns and interests of the Australian Jewish community to key political, media, and civil society stakeholders. As a theory, a base strategy is useful for explaining how a cause-oriented group uses ideological commitment as the glue that binds together its support base.

Finally, AIJAC has participated in pro-Israel public diplomacy and nation branding on both formal and informal levels. Formal public diplomacy has consisted of hosting official bilateral functions and meetings between Australian and Israeli leaders and policy-makers. Informal public diplomacy and nation branding has taken the form of producing pro-Israel communications output through its own platform and other media publishers and platforms, hosting Israeli and pro-Israel guest speakers, and organising information trips to Israel to promote Israeli culture, heritage, and identity and manage Israel's image.

References

ABC News24. (2017, January 13). *AIJAC's Jamie Hyams on Israeli settlements and Jerusalem*. AIJAC – Australia/Israel & Jewish Affairs Council. https://aijac.org.au/update/video-aijac-s-jamie-hyams-on-israeli-settlements/

ACNC. (2019, December 18). *AIJAC governing document*. https://acncpubfile-sprodstorage.blob.core.windows.net/public/0dc70a0b-4641-e911-a978-00 0d3ad0574c-475a57f9-22e8-4b77-8ea9-3aa24d2cbdab-Governing%20 Document-407c5ed9-1b21-ea11-a810-000d3ad1cc03-CONSTITUTION_-_AUSTRALIA_ISRAEL__JEWISH_AFFAIRS_ COUNCIL_(003).pdf

ACNC. (n.d.). *Australia/Israel & Jewish Affairs Council*. Retrieved August 26, 2020, from https://www.acnc.gov.au/charity/00929e2ff28489006ce226f2a caaf60d#overview

Ahmed, T. (2016, June). When Muslim Antisemitism comes to Australia. *Australia/Israel Review 41*(6). https://aijac.org.au/australia-israel-review/when-muslim-antisemitism-comes-to-australia/

AIJAC. (n.d.). *About AIJAC*. Retrieved August 15, 2019, from https://aijac.org.au/about-aijac/

AIJAC. (2010, June 1). *Factsheet: The Gaza Flotilla*. https://aijac.org.au/resource/factsheet-the-gaza-flotilla/

AIJAC. (2012a, December 5). *Foreign Minister's focus on Israeli settlements "misplaced" and "counter-productive*.https://aijac.org.au/media-release/foreign-minister-s-focus-on-israeli-settlements/

AIJAC [@AIJAC_Update]. (2012b, January 9). *Palestinian rights activist confirms Hamas puts terror bases in civilian areas*. https://twitter.com/AIJAC_Update/statuses/156591459280232448

AIJAC [@AIJAC_Update]. (2012c, April 10). *Easter in Jerusalem*. https://twitter.com/AIJAC_Update/statuses/189962871818555392

AIJAC. (2012d, December 6). *Australia's Woodside Petroleum goes to Israel*. https://www.facebook.com/297825343569944/posts/505921962775717/

AIJAC. (2014a, February 6). *Ehud Yaari to speak in Melbourne and Sydney*. https://aijac.org.au/media-release/ehud-yaari-to-speak-in-melbourne-and-sydney/

AIJAC [@AIJAC_Update]. (2014b, November 11). *Priest tells UN: Israel is the "only safe place" for Christians in the Middle East: Today Christians are the m....* https://twitter.com/AIJAC_Update/statuses/532391942756118528

AIJAC. (2014c, November 28). *Israel in a collapsing middle east: Changes, threats & opportunities*. https://www.facebook.com/297825343569944/posts/903601712992301/

AIJAC [@AIJAC_Update]. (2014d, December 8). *"At Israel's MIT, Arab women (and men) are suddenly thriving" via @BW*. https://twitter.com/AIJAC_Update/statuses/542173019402031104

AIJAC. (2015a, July 23). *Key points against unilateral Palestinian recognition*. https://aijac.org.au/resource/key-points-against-unilateral-palestinian-recogn/.

AIJAC [@AIJAC_Update]. (2015b, June 3). *@MalBrough_MP & Sen @SeanC_Edwards recently joined AIJAC in Sydney to report on their Ramban study visit*

to #Israel. https://twitter.com/AIJAC_Update/statuses/606330563
394301952
AIJAC [@AIJAC_Update]. (2015c, October 29). *Meet the Jewish doctor who saves Palestinian attackers & the Muslim doctor who saves Jewish victims @washingtonpost.* https://twitter.com/AIJAC_Update/statuses/658834188099936256
AIJAC. (2015d, January 21). *'Not condemning Antisemitism only fuels extremism' - AIJAC's Glen Falkenstein on ABC'S The Drum on the attacks in France, extremism and the status of French Jewry.* Facebook. https://www.facebook.com/297825343569944/posts/938676916151447/
AIJAC. (2015e, February 2). *Editorial: Normalising the Unacceptable.* https://www.facebook.com/297825343569944/posts/946044608748011/
AIJAC. (2015f, September 24). IsraAID has assisted 31 countries in disaster relief, and now its volunteers are helping refugees in Europe. https://www.facebook.com/297825343569944/posts/1073732322645905/.
AIJAC. (2015g, October 26). *The Jewish community leadership met with Opposition leader bill shorten MP and his parliamentary colleagues Mark Dreyfus MP and Michael Danby MP, to discuss the ALP's approach to Israel and other issues of concern to the community.* https://www.facebook.com/297825343569944/posts/1087835824568888/
AIJAC. (2015h, December 2). *Israel will inaugurate for the first time an official – and visible – diplomatic mission in Abu Dhabi, capital of the United Arab Emirates, in the coming weeks.* https://www.facebook.com/297825343569944/posts/1105330886152715/
AIJAC. (2016a, March 10). *"Confronting BDS 'macro-aggression' on campus", in this month's Australia/Israel Review.* https://www.facebook.com/297825343569944/posts/1163368453682291/
AIJAC. (2016b, March 29). *AIJAC's meeting with Prime Minister Malcolm Turnbull in the The Australian Jewish News.* https://www.facebook.com/297825343569944/posts/1179979108687892/
AIJAC. (2016c, April 8). *Great news: New joint R&D agreement signed by NSW Premier Mike Baird & Israelâ€™s Office of Chief Scientist #innovation Read more about the agreement here.* https://www.facebook.com/297825343569944/posts/1188236744528795/
AIJAC. (2016d, May 13). *"Pollies report back on Israel trip" following one of AIJAC's recent Rambam missions - from this week's Australian Jewish News.* https://www.facebook.com/297825343569944/posts/1211507388868397/
AIJAC [@AIJAC_Update]. (2016e, June 6). *Materials have been found in Palestinian textbooks breaching PA pledges to halt anti-Israel incitement in schools.* https://twitter.com/AIJAC_Update/statuses/740027878876667905
AIJAC [@AIJAC_Update]. (2016f, July 5). *No place for #PaulineHanson's & #OneNation's destructive rhetoric #racism #bigotry #auspol @MrJeremyJones @Jwire.* https://twitter.com/AIJAC_Update/statuses/750525697299402753

AIJAC [@AIJAC_Update]. (2016, August 21). *AIJAC's Executive Director Colin Rubenstein quoted in this week's Australian Jewish News*. https://twitter.com/AIJAC_Update/statuses/767544758486958081

AIJAC. (2016h, November 4). *'Major Israeli military and public figures addressed an AIJAC luncheon in Sydney as well as a public event at Sydney's Central Synagogue on Wednesday following their participation in the 2016 Australia/Israel Military to Military Dialogue (the Be'er Sheva Dialogue)*. https://www.facebook.com/297825343569944/posts/1355713451114456/

AIJAC. (2016i, November 7). *AIJAC National Chairman Mark Leibler meets with Israeli PM Netanyahu*. https://aijac.org.au/media-release/aijac-national-chairman-mark-leibler-meets-with/

AIJAC. (2016j, November 22). *Israeli Minister to speak in Melbourne, Sydney*. https://aijac.org.au/media-release/israeli-minister-to-speak-in-melbourne-sydney/

AIJAC. (2017a, January 31). *A group of Islamic leaders and educators from Indonesia, accompanied by AIJAC's Jeremy Jones, has completed an eight day mission of dialogue, study and mutual learning in Israel and the Palestinian Authority*. https://www.facebook.com/297825343569944/posts/1455215347830932/

AIJAC. (2017b, March 17). *AIJAC's involvement in Israeli Prime Minister Netanyahu's historic visit to Australia*. https://aijac.org.au/update/aijac-s-involvement-in-israeli-prime-minister-ne/

AIJAC [@AIJAC_Update]. (2017c, March 26). *How Project Rozana is giving hope to sick Palestinian kids and their families*. https://twitter.com/AIJAC_Update/statuses/846143360247238659

AIJAC [@AIJAC_Update]. (2017d, April 25). *Breakthrough for Muslim women in Israel...* https://twitter.com/AIJAC_Update/status/857036446850363392

AIJAC. (2017e, June 9). *Three recent graduates of the Rambam Israel Study Tour were guests at an AIJAC luncheon hosted in Melbourne today....* https://www.facebook.com/297825343569944/posts/1596525513699914/

AIJAC. (2017f, July 1). *Trade Unionists and Rambam returnees recently addressed an AIJAC luncheon in Melbourne following their return from Israel J-Wire*. https://www.facebook.com/297825343569944/posts/1621917837827348/.

AIJAC [@AIJAC_Update]. (2017g, August 15). *Inside a major Australian #Agtech Mission to Israel - designed and delivered by Austrade @catalyst_au ...* https://twitter.com/AIJAC_Update/statuses/897662185584959488

AIJAC. (2017h, November 9). *Prime Minister Turnbull addressed Beersheba Dialogue event co-hosted by AIJAC*. https://aijac.org.au/media-release/prime-minister-turnbull-addressed-beersheba-dial/

AIJAC [@AIJAC_Update]. (2017j, December 14). *National Council of Students passes long overdue resolution to combat antisemitism and make Jewish students feel welcome on Australian university campuses*. https://twitter.com/AIJAC_Update/statuses/941542713232646144.

AIJAC. (2017j, December 19). *If ... the Palestinian leader is unwilling to acknowledge the justice of Israel's historical claim to the land, will he ever be able make true peace? Or has Abbas finally and definitively disqualified himself—as Arafat did in 2002—as an interlocutor of peace with Israel?.* https://www.facebook.com/297825343569944/posts/1800274083325055/

AIJAC. (2018a, January 10). Terrible news—"Israeli father of 6, MDA volunteer medic killed in drive-by shooting terror attack near Nablus. https://www.facebook.com/297825343569944/posts/1823157754370021/.

AIJAC [@AIJAC_Update]. (2018b, February 14). *A Palestinian diplomat speaking to students at the United Nations headquarters in New York told them the Palestinians were proud to be throwing stones at Israeli forces and will continue teaching their children to do so.* https://twitter.com/AIJAC_Update/statuses/964020742139478016

AIJAC. (2018c, February 21). *Don't miss Dr. Daniel Pipes' talk in Melbourne on "Winners and losers in a fractured Middle East" on Feb. 27 - check the flyer for further details.* https://www.facebook.com/297825343569944/posts/1868242726528190/

AIJAC. (2018e, May 1). *The footage also offers a glimpse into how protesters who damaged the fence walked away with parts they dismantled and flew incendiary kites into the sky in an effort to torch agricultural land on the Israeli side of the border.* https://www.facebook.com/297825343569944/posts/1942877629064699/

AIJAC. (2018d, April 30). *Former IDF spokesperson to speak in Melbourne.* https://aijac.org.au/media-release/former-idf-spokesperson-to-speak-in-melbourne/

AIJAC. (2018g, June 5). *AIJAC writes to the ABC asking it to explain the lack of coverage of Gaza rocket attacks.* https://aijac.org.au/media-release/aijac-writes-to-the-abc-asking-it-to-explain-the/

AIJAC [@AIJAC_Update]. (2018g, June 11). An Israeli medical team dispatched to Guatemala last week to treat victims of a devastating volcano there were using a special enzyme developed at the Soroka-University Medical Center in Beersheba to treat the wounded. https://twitter.com/AIJAC_Update/statuses/1006372937383833600.

AIJAC. (2018h, June 14). *AIJAC thanks Australian government for principled stance at UN.* https://aijac.org.au/media-release/aijac-thanks-australian-government-for-principled-stance-at-un/

AIJAC. (2018i, July 18). *A rocket fired from Gaza hit a Sderot playground on Saturday. Fortunately all the children had been evacuated beforehand.* https://www.facebook.com/297825343569944/posts/2044195522266242/

AIJAC. (2018j, August 6). *AIJAC complains to ABC on Hamas Description; Wins complaints on SBS Arabic story.* https://aijac.org.au/media-release/aijac-complains-to-abc-on-hamas-description-wins-complaint-on-sbs-arabic-story/

AIJAC. (2018t, May 17). A #Hamas official on Wednesday acknowledged that 50 of the 62 Palestinians reported killed during Gaza border riots on Monday and Tuesday were members of the Islamist terrorist group. https://www.facebook.com/297825343569944/posts/1960559940629801/.

Asa-El, A. (2012, December). The Rockets of November. *Australia/Israel Review* 37(12). https://aijac.org.au/australia-israel-review/the-rockets-of-november/

Asa-El, A. (2014, August). Gaza War – Again. *Australia/Israel Review* 39(8). https://aijac.org.au/australia-israel-review/gaza-war-again/

Asa-El, A. (2018, May). A stunning economic success story. *Australia/Israel Review* 43(5). https://aijac.org.au/australia-israel-review/a-stunning-economic-success-story/

Avi-Guy, O. (2013, May 20). *A Teen's Life in Gaza – Terrorism training, with beatings for anyone sporting "cool" haircuts or skinny jeans*. AIJAC. https://aijac.org.au/update/a-teen-s-life-in-gaza-terrorism-training-with-be/

Bartle, J., & Griffiths, D. (2002). Social-psychological, economic and marketing models of voting behaviour compared. In N. J. O'Shaughnessy & S. C. M. Henneberg (Eds.), *The idea of political marketing* (pp. 19–37). Praeger.

Bassem Eid on prospects for a Palestinian state. (2015, August 27). AIJAC. https://aijac.org.au/update/video-bassem-eid-on-prospects-for-a-palestinian/.

Beroff, R. (2017, June 16). *BDS versus Wonder Woman*. AIJAC. https://aijac.org.au/update/bds-versus-wonder-woman/

Burack, G. (2018, 11 June). *Will international pressure end pay for slay?*. AIJAC. https://aijac.org.au/fresh-air/will-international-pressure-end-pay-for-slay/

Corey Wingard MP (South Australia) – Impressions of Israel [Video]. (2017, March 31). AIJAC. https://aijac.org.au/update/video-corey-wingard-mp-south-australia-impressio/

Debinski, G., & Shapiro, A. (2014, November 18). *The Fictional Basis of Carr's Palestine pivot*. AIJAC. https://aijac.org.au/update/the-fictional-basis-of-carrs-palestine-pivot/

Falkenstein, G. (2014, July 25). *Hamas makes civilian casualties a tragic certainty*. AIJAC. https://aijac.org.au/op-ed/hamas-makes-civilian-casualties-a-tragic-certain/

Falkenstein, G. (2015, March 17). *Antisemitism on Campus: Has Sydney University's Jake Lynch finally gone too far?*. AIJAC. https://aijac.org.au/update/antisemitism-on-campus-has-sydney-university-s-j/

Falkenstein, G. & Narunsky, G. (2016, July). Politically right, but very wrong. *Australia/Israel Review* 41(7). https://aijac.org.au/australia-israel-review/politically-right-but-very-wrong/

Fleischer, T. (2012, November). Scribblings: Body counts and proportionality. *Australia/Israel Review* 37(12). https://aijac.org.au/australia-israel-review/scribblings-body-counts-and-proportionality/

Fleischer, T. (2013, January). Scribblings: What Palestinians want. *AIR – Australia/Israel Review 38*(1). https://aijac.org.au/australia-israel-review/scribblings-what-palestinians-want/

Fleischer, T. (2016, October). Scribblings: Article 49(6) and the settlements. *Australia/Israel Review 41*(10). https://aijac.org.au/australia-israel-review/scribblings-article-49-6-and-the-settlements/

Fleischer, T. (2017, September 4). *The "targeting" and "pressure" that so annoyed John Lyons.* AIJAC. https://aijac.org.au/update/the-targeting-and-pressure-that-so-annoyed-john/

Fleischer, T. (2018, April 17). *Myths and facts about Gaza's march of return.* AIJAC. https://aijac.org.au/op-ed/myths-and-facts-about-gazas-march-of-return/.

Gawenda, M. (2020). *The power broker: Mark Leibler, an Australian Jewish life.* Monash University Press.

Han, E., & Rane, H. (2013). *Making Australian foreign policy on Israel-Palestine: Media coverage, public opinion and interest groups. Islamic studies series.* (Book 13). Melbourne University Press.

Hyams, J. (2011, May). Media microscope: ANU Blues. *Australia/Israel Review, 36*(5). https://aijac.org.au/australia-israel-review/media-microscope-anu-blues/

Hyams, J. (2014, December 8). *Letter to The Age/SMH: Home demolitions.* AIJAC. https://aijac.org.au/op-ed/letter-to-the-age-smh-home-demolitions/

Jones, J. (2016, March). The last word: Opening eyes. *Australia/Israel Review 41*(3). https://aijac.org.au/australia-israel-review/the-last-word-opening-eyes/.

Jones, J. (2018, May). The last word: Return engagement. *Australia/Israel Review 43*(5). https://aijac.org.au/australia-israel-review/the-last-word-return-engagement/

Lee, A. (2015a, June 11). *Sophie's house of cards.* AIJAC. https://aijac.org.au/update/sophie-s-house-of-cards/

Lee, A. (2015b, June 18). *Gaza casualties: Israeli report refutes widely cited UN figures.* AIJAC. https://aijac.org.au/update/gaza-casualties-israeli-report-refutes-widely-ci/

Lee, A. (2015c, December 4). *ABC's Sophie McNeill tackles incitement, doubles down on insistence that "occupation" behind terror.* AIJAC. https://aijac.org.au/update/abc-s-sophie-mcneill-tackles-incitement-doubles/

Lees-Marshment, J. (2004). *The political marketing revolution: Transforming the government of the UK.* Manchester University Press.

Lerman, E. (2017, August 11). *South Australian politicians have made right decision voting against unilateral recognition of Palestine.* AIJAC. https://aijac.org.au/op-ed/south-australian-politicians-have-made-right-dec/

Levey, G. B., & Mendes, P. (2004). The Hanan Ashrawi affair: Australian Jewish politics on display. In G. B. Levey & P. Mendes (Eds.), *Jews and Australian politics* (pp. 215–230). Sussex Academic Press.

Levin, S. (2017, March 8). *Beyond the photo-opportunities: The concrete results of Netanyahu's visit to Australia*. AIJAC. https://aijac.org.au/fresh-air/beyond-the-photo-opportunities-the-concrete-resu/

Loewenstein, A. (2006). *My Israel Question*. Melbourne University Press.

Lyons, J. (2017). *Balcony over Jerusalem*. Harper Collins Publishers Australia.

Mendes, P. (2016). An updated history of the Australian Jewish Democratic Society, 2000–16. *Australian Jewish Historical Society Journal, 23*(1), 111–148. https://research.monash.edu/files/16004432/AJDS_History_pdf.

Meyerowitz-Katz, D. (2011, August 27). *Boycotters' free expression costs businesses plenty*. AIJAC. https://aijac.org.au/op-ed/boycotters-free-expression-costs-businesses-plen/

Meyerowitz-Katz, D. (2012a, May 22). *Striking prisoners are no Gandhi-esque resisters*. AIJAC. https://aijac.org.au/op-ed/striking-prisoners-are-no-gandhi-esque-resisters/

Meyerowitz-Katz, D. (2012b, November 2). *Younger Israeli Arabs see engagement, not hostility, as path to equality*. AIJAC. https://aijac.org.au/update/younger-israeli-arabs-see-engagement-not-hostili/

Meyerowitz-Katz, D. (2012c, December 28). *Friends and enemies colour BDS ideology*. AIJAC. https://aijac.org.au/op-ed/friends-and-enemies-colour-bds-ideology/

Mittelman, S. (2012, June 1). Israel returns bodies of 91 Palestinians, in goodwill gesture. AIJAC. https://aijac.org.au/update/israel-returns-bodies-of-91-palestinians-in-good/

Mittelman, S. (2013, August 29). *ALP, Coalition offer answers to key policy question for the Jewish Community*. AIJAC. https://aijac.org.au/op-ed/alp-coalition-offer-answers-to-key-policy-questi/

Mittelman, S. (2015a, July 24). *Carr's offensive ANU speech*. AIJAC. https://aijac.org.au/update/carr-s-offensive-anu-speech/

Mittelman, S. (2015b, April). Deconstruction Zone: Delegitimisation/Settlement Blues. *Australia/Israel Review 40*(4). https://aijac.org.au/australia-israel-review/deconstruction-zone-delegitimisation-settlement/

Mittelman, S. (2015c, November 4). Who is really challenging the "status quo" in Jerusalem?. AIJAC. https://aijac.org.au/update/who-is-really-challenging-the-status-quo-in-jeru/.

Mittelman, S. (2016, April). Lucy in the sky – and down to earth. *Australia/Israel Review 41*(4). https://aijac.org.au/australia-israel-review/lucy-in-the-sky-and-down-to-earth/.

Mittelman, S. (2018, April 3). *Australia should fund Palestinian welfare, but not pay to slay*. AIJAC. https://aijac.org.au/op-ed/australia-should-fund-palestinian-welfare-but-no/

Narunsky, G. (2012, March 1). *Israel wows Coalition lawmakers*. AIJAC. https://aijac.org.au/media-release/israel-wows-coalition-lawmakers/

Narunsky, G. (2017, March 8). *"Settlements Bob" At It Again: A fisking*. AIJAC. https://aijac.org.au/update/settlements-bob-at-it-again-a-fisking/

Ostrovsky, A. (2011, May 13). *Gillard shouldn't give our money to terrorists.* AIJAC. https://aijac.org.au/op-ed/gillard-shouldn-t-give-our-money-to-terrorists/

Pettitt, R. T. (2015). Internal part political relationship marketing: Encouraging activism amongst local party members. In J. Lees-Marshment (Ed.), *Routledge handbook of political marketing* (pp. 137–150). Routledge.

Porat, R. (2018a, January). The Dark Side of Arabic media. *Australia/Israel Review* 43(1). https://aijac.org.au/australia-israel-review/the-dark-side-of-arabic-media/.

Porat, R. (2018b, July). Extremism – by the Book. *Australia/Israel Review* 43(7). https://aijac.org.au/australia-israel-review/extremism-by-the-book/

Reich, C. (2004). Inside AIJAC – An Australian Jewish Lobby Group. In G. B. Levey & P. Mendes (Eds.), *Jews and Australian politics* (pp. 198–214). Sussex Academic Press.

Rubenstein, C. (2011, November). Editorial: An extraordinary society. *Australia/Israel Review, 36*(11). https://aijac.org.au/australia-israel-review/editorial-an-extraordinary-society/

Rubenstein, C. (2014, June 24). *Letter: Foggy thinking on Israel's "occupation.* AIJAC. https://aijac.org.au/op-ed/letter-foggy-thinking-on-israel-s-occupation/

Rubenstein, C. (2016a, January). Editorial: Israeli Innovation Inspires. *Australia/Israel Review* 41(1). https://aijac.org.au/australia-israel-review/editorial-israeli-innovation-inspires/

Rubenstein, C. (2016b, September). Editorial: Lessons of the Gaza scandal. *Australia/Israel Review* 41(9). https://aijac.org.au/australia-israel-review/editorial-lessons-of-the-gaza-scandal/

Rubenstein, C. (2017a, January 4). *Two-state outcome damaged by the United Nations Security Council Resolution 2334.* AIJAC. https://aijac.org.au/op-ed/two-state-outcome-damaged-by-united-nations-secu/

Rubenstein, C. (2017b, December 17). *Recognising Jerusalem as Israel's capital is a welcome, symbolic move.* AIJAC. https://aijac.org.au/op-ed/recognising-jerusalem-as-israel-s-capital-is-a-w/

Rubenstein, C. (2018a, March 23). *The misguided campaign against visiting Middle East expert Daniel Pipes.* AIJAC. https://aijac.org.au/update/the-misguided-campaign-against-visiting-middle-e/

Rubenstein, C. (2018b, May 14). *Israel's success story will have more chapters.* AIJAC. https://aijac.org.au/op-ed/israel-s-success-story-will-have-more-chapters/

Rubenstein, C. (2018c, August 3). *Myths and Facts about Israel's controversial new Nation-State law.* AIJAC. https://aijac.org.au/op-ed/myths-and-facts-about-israels-controversial-new-nation-state-law/

Rubenstein, C. (2018d, June). Editorial: Tragedy and truth in Gaza. *Australia/Israel Review* 43(6). https://aijac.org.au/australia-israel-review/editorial-tragedy-and-truth-in-gaza/

SBS World News. (2018, August 6). Dr Colin Rubenstein on Israel's Nation-State law – SBS World News. *AIJAC – Australia/Israel & Jewish Affairs Council*. https://aijac.org.au/video/dr-colin-rubenstein-on-israels-nation-state-law-sbs-world-news/

Shapiro, A. (2012, March 9). *Israel makes inroads in Asia with a diplomatic "Ace in the Hole" – Water and Agricultural Technology*. AIJAC. https://aijac.org.au/update/israel-makes-inroads-in-asia-with-a-diplomatic-a/

Shapiro, A. (2013, September 11). New revelations about Israel's help for victims of Syrian civil war. AIJAC. https://aijac.org.au/update/new-revelations-about-israel-s-help-for-victims/.

Shapiro, A. (2015, March 13). *Should the ABC have given advocacy journalist Sophie McNeill the keys to its Jerusalem bureau*. AIJAC. https://aijac.org.au/update/should-the-abc-have-given-advocacy-journalist-so/

Shapiro, A. (2016a, September 29). *Part 1: Crossing Erez – Another Gazan smear of Israel from ABC's McNeill*. AIJAC. https://aijac.org.au/update/part-1-crossing-erez-another-gazan-smear-of-isra/

Shapiro, A. (2016b, September 29). *Part 2: Crossing Erez – Another Gazan smear of Israel from ABC's McNeill*. AIJAC. https://aijac.org.au/update/part-2-crossing-erez-another-gazan-smear-of-isra/

Shapiro, A. (2016c, July). The Greens and Israel. *Australia/Israel Review 41*(7). https://aijac.org.au/australia-israel-review/the-greens-and-israel/

Shapiro, A. (2017a, May 5). *Five stand-outs about Hamas' new policy manifesto*. AIJAC. https://aijac.org.au/update/five-stand-outs-about-hamas-new-policy-manifesto/

Shapiro, A. (2017b, August 15). *Former Netanyahu advisor Lerman discusses Israel's true settlement strategy*. AIJAC. https://aijac.org.au/update/former-netanyahu-advisor-lerman-discusses-israel/

Shapiro, A. (2017c, November 17). *How to Understand John Lyons' memoir Balcony Over Jerusalem*. AIJAC. https://aijac.org.au/update/how-to-understand-john-lyons-memoir-balcony-over/

Shapiro, A. (2017d, December). Back to Beersheba. *Australia/Israel Review 42*(12). https://aijac.org.au/australia-israel-review/back-to-beersheba/

Sky News AM Agenda. (2018, May 16). *Jamie Hyams on Gaza border violence*. AIJAC. https://aijac.org.au/op-ed/video-jamie-hyams-on-gaza-border-violence/

The Face-Off. (2013, September). *Australia/Israel Review 38*(9). https://aijac.org.au/australia-israel-review/the-face-off/

Yosef Abramowitz on Israel's green energy outreach, human rights and environmental activism. (2018, May 1). AIJAC. https://aijac.org.au/video/yosef-abramowitz-on-israels-green-energy-outreach-human-rights-and-environmental-activism/

CHAPTER 5

Australia Palestine Advocacy Network

Abstract This chapter explores the political marketing, public diplomacy, and nation branding activities of the Australia Palestine Advocacy Network (APAN), a national coalition of pro-Palestinian groups and individuals seeking to influence Australian public policy towards the Palestinians and Israel. It draws upon a content analysis of webpages, magazine articles, op-ed columns, videos, and social media posts produced by APAN between 2010 and 2018. These primary sources were supplemented by an interview with APAN's Executive Officer Jessica Morrison. This chapter will give a brief description of the group before discussing the group's market-orientation, "segmentation, targeting, and position" (STP), internal marketing, public diplomacy, and nation branding strategies and activities.

Keywords Palestinian solidarity • BDS (Boycott, Divestment, and Sanctions) • Product-orientation • Segments • Base strategy • Public diplomacy

© The Author(s), under exclusive license to Springer Nature Switzerland AG 2022
A. Lim, *Political Marketing and Public Diplomacy by Pro-Israel and Pro-Palestinian Advocacy Groups*, Palgrave Studies in Political Marketing and Management,
https://doi.org/10.1007/978-3-031-15332-7_5

Overview

The Australia Palestine Advocacy Network is a national coalition of pro-Palestinian advocacy organisations and individuals, formed in 2011. APAN's key aims and goals have included promoting Palestinian rights and self-determination; ending the Israeli military occupation, settlement expansion, and the blockade of the Palestinian Territories; promoting a "just and lasting" negotiated solution to the Israel-Palestine conflict in accordance with international law; and building alliances with like-minded Palestinian solidarity groups and activists in Australia and abroad. APAN's membership consists of human rights groups, Jewish and Palestinian groups, aid and development agencies, and trade unions. The Network is led by an Executive with key members including President George Browning (a retired Anglican Bishop) and Vice-President Nasser Mashni, who also helped to establish the Australians for Palestine and Olive Kids advocacy groups (APAN, n.d.-a, n.d.-b).

Marketing Orientation

The content analysis generated little information about APAN's marketing orientation. A March 2014 Twitter post reporting on APAN's meetings with Australian politicians shows that the organisation engages in campaign delivery by informing supporters of their achievements (APAN, 2014c). A 2018 informational Vimeo video suggests that APAN is a product-oriented advocacy group since it was founded to advance Palestinian rights and self-determination. APAN has also made efforts to recruit like-minded members, volunteers, and financial donors (APAN, 2018i). Morrison (personal communication, April 7, 2020) stated that APAN used its media releases, website, and public gatherings to attract individuals and groups who were interested or involved in Palestinian human rights and justice as well as human rights in general. Taken together, the content analysis and Morrison's interview show that APAN pursues a product-orientation. As a product-oriented advocacy group, APAN would focus on "battling for their cause and not on changing their behaviour to suit membership subscriptions, public or government opinion. They may believe that as long as they all work towards a common goal, people will simply see how good they are and support them automatically, and they will be able to influence government" (Lees-Marshment, 2004, pp. 97–98). As Table 5.1 shows, APAN followed the four stages of a product-oriented charity/advocacy group:

Table 5.1 APAN analysed using Lees-Marshment's product-oriented framework

Stages	Definitions	Examples
Product design	Design a wide range of behaviour according to what it thinks is right, and assume it will succeed, "do good" and achieve its goals, as well as raise enough money to do this.	Advancing Palestinian rights and self-determination; seeks to end the Israeli military occupation, settlement expansion, and the Gaza Blockade and supports the Boycott, Divestment and Sanctions (BDS) Movement, a "just and lasting" solution to the Israel-Palestine conflict within the framework of international law (APAN, n.d.-a, n.d.-b, 2011a, 2016i; Shaik, 2015).
Communication	Information is there if people want to get it.	Promoting its advocacy work through its website, media releases, public gatherings, social media, and op-ed columns and letters, and media interviews (Morrison, personal communication, April 7, 2020).
Campaign	Inform and lobby individuals, groups, governments, and other actors about what they want. This may also include short-term campaigns.	Working with individuals and organisations that share its commitment to Palestinian human rights and self-determination. Lobbying a range of political, media, and civil society actors (Morrison, personal communication, April 7, 2020).
Delivery	Deliver what they think is best.	Using its website, social media, and email newsletters to inform people of their work and achievements (Morrison, personal communication, April 7, 2020; APAN, 2014c, 2016a).

Analysis

In terms of marketing orientation, APAN fulfilled the four criteria of a "product-oriented advocacy group" in the Lees-Marshment "product/sales/market orientation" model. First, APAN has a clear product (Palestinian rights and self-determination) which it is unwilling to change to suit elite or public opinion. Second, APAN has promoted this product through its communications output and advocacy activities. Third, APAN has engaged in campaigning by networking with like-minded groups and activists in Australia and abroad as well as lobbying key stakeholders in Australian society. Finally, APAN has used its communications output to inform supporters and the public about their achievements.

Segmentation, Targeting, and Positioning (STP)

Segmentation

Morrison (personal communication, April 7, 2020) claimed that APAN did not conduct segmentation but "attracted people who were concerned with human rights as a general paradigm including Palestinian rights." However, the Network's website's "Palestine in Australian politics" reports and their petition campaigns during the 2013 and 2016 Australian federal elections showed that they have conducted research to identify political segments who are sympathetic to the Palestinians and the Network's work. While these webpages are no longer available, they generated useful insights into how the Network segmented and targeted sympathetic Australian political parties and politicians. Despite their usefulness, they generated no information about APAN's efforts to segment and target various civil society actors including activists, NGOs, ethnic and faith communities, businesses, and trade unions, leaving a gap that future studies can help address. This section looks at three case studies: APAN's "Palestine in Australian Politics" reports and its advocacy campaigns during the 2013 and 2016 federal elections.

Palestine in Australian Politics, 2011–2018

Seeking to influence Australian foreign policy towards Israel-Palestine, APAN has collected statements by Australian parliamentarians on Palestine and lobbied Australian politicians during the 2013 and 2016 federal elections. Between 2011 and 2018, APAN has monitored parliamentary debates and speeches for references to Palestine through its annual "Palestine in Australian Politics" reports (APAN, 2011b, 2012d, 2013f, 2014g, 2014l, 2015c, 2015i, 2016d, 2016j, 2018a, 2018g). These parliamentary reports generated several observations:

1. First, the Australian Greens were the staunchest pro-Palestinian supporters in the Australian Parliament with the most vocal voices including Senators Lee Rhiannon, Scott Ludlam, and party leader Richard Di Natale.
2. Second, the Australian Labor Party (ALP) contained both pro-Palestinian and pro-Israel supporters. Notable pro-Palestinian Labor parliamentarians have included Maria Vamvakinou, Melissa Parke, Jill Hall, Ross Hart, Tony Zappia, and Anne Urquhart. Meanwhile

pro-Israel Labor parliamentarians have included Michael Danby, Milton Dick, and Mike Kelly.
3. Third, while most Coalition parliamentarians particularly Liberal Senator Eric Abetz were pro-Israel and hostile to Palestinian interests, there were several exceptions including Liberal MPs Sussan Levy, Russell Broadbent, and Craig Laundy, and National Party of Australia (NPA) MP Mark Coulton.
4. Fourth, independent Senator Nick Xenophon and his former "Nick Xenophon Team" (now known as Centre Alliance) were also sympathetic to the Palestinians.
5. Finally, several minor parties like Pauline Hanson's One Nation Party and the libertarian Liberal Democratic Party made remarks attacking Muslims and Palestinian leader Mahmoud Abbas respectively.

Together, these observations show that APAN has sought to cultivate relations with sympathetic Australian politicians and parties in order to influence Australian foreign policy towards Israel-Palestine. While the left-wing Greens and Labor parties were the most sympathetic to the Palestinians, APAN is interested in building cross-party support as shown by the presence of sympathetic Coalition MPs like Laundy and Coulton.

2013 Australian Federal Election
The content analysis showed that APAN used segmentation and targeting when lobbying political candidates during the 2013 Australian federal election. During the 2013 federal election, APAN got their supporters to send postcards and emails to political candidates from various parties asking them their position on several questions relating to Australian foreign towards the Palestinians' "struggle for freedom," which are outlined below:

- Did your party support Palestine's bid for the United Nations membership in November 2012?
- Does your party support a peace settlement based upon the 1967 borders?
- What is your party's position on the Jewish settlements in the Occupied Palestinian Territories?
- What is your party's position on Israel's blockade of the Gaza Strip?
- What is your party's position regarding aid to Palestine?

- If you are elected, will you advocate for an Australian Foreign Policy that supports the Palestinian's struggle for freedom and independence? (Storey, 2013)

APAN received responses from 44 politicians. Based on these responses, APAN stated its positions on the Coalition (Liberal/National), Labor, and Green parties' policies towards Israel-Palestine:

- APAN criticised the Coalition's opposition to Palestinian admission into the United Nations General Assembly (UNGA) and BDS campaign, and its promise to strengthen relations with Israel, which it viewed as at odds with international opinion in the light of alleged Israeli intransigence towards the Palestinians. While Liberal and National candidates reiterated their parties' support for a two-state solution, they tended to side with Israel, blaming the conflict on the Palestinians.
- While APAN welcomed Labor's support for a two-state solution based on the 1967 border (or Green Line) and opposition to illegal Jewish settlements in the West Bank, it disagreed with the party's abstention on the granting of non-member observer status to the Palestinians at the UNGA. While most Labor candidates tended to toe their party's policies, some Labor candidates like Michael Stove and Melissa Parke supported the removal of Jewish settlers from the West Bank and condemned the Gaza Blockade, issues not mentioned in Labor's platform (Stove, 2013; Parke, 2013).
- APAN (2013b, 2013c) also praised the Greens for supporting Palestinian rights and aspiration, upgrading Palestine's UN membership status, and opposing Israel's bombing and blockade of Gaza, and settlement expansion in the West Bank and East Jerusalem. The researcher found that Green candidates were most sympathetic to the Palestinians.

The content analysis found that Green and Labor candidates had a higher response rate to APAN's survey than Coalition MPs, who comprise less than 20% of respondents. This suggests that left-wing politicians and parties are more sympathetic to Palestinian solidarity groups than right-wing ones.

2016 Australian Federal Election

APAN also used segmentation and targeting when lobbying political candidates during the 2016 Australian federal election. APAN got its supporters to email political candidates, asking them to sign APAN's Pledge:

1. I unequivocally support the equal rights of Palestinians and Israelis to live in peace within internationally recognised and secure borders, in accordance with relevant United Nations resolutions and international and humanitarian laws.
2. Ensure if I travel to the region, I will spend equal time observing the facts on the ground and listening to Palestinian voices as to Israeli voices.
3. Publicly advocate for Australia to join 136 countries (70% of the world) to recognise Palestine and to call for an end to the occupation.
4. Support nonviolent activities that help to achieve these goals and provide hope for a just and peaceful resolution (Morrison, personal communication, December 9, 2019).

APAN received 127 responses, which amounted to roughly 10% of candidates contesting that election (APAN, 2017a). APAN (2016f, 2016g) also evaluated 11 political parties' policies and positions towards the Palestinians. Key findings are outlined below:

- 58 respondents signed APAN's pledge including all 51 Green candidates, 8 Labor candidates, 2 Socialist Alliance candidates, and the candidates from the Nick Xenophon Team, the Australian Defence Veterans Party, and the Animal Justice Party.
- Coalition: Despite the Coalition's claim to support a two-state solution, APAN disagreed with their aid policies and their support for a negotiated peaceful resolution without "any preconditions," which APAN felt favoured Israel. APAN was dissatisfied with the Coalition's lack of interest in Israel settlements in the West Bank, travel to Palestine, and human rights abuses but praised their belated recognition of Palestinian rights.
- Labor: APAN criticised their lack of engagement on spending equal time in Palestine, unclear position on Israeli settlements, and opposition to BDS. However, APAN praised the Labor Party for its openness to recognising Palestinian statehood.

- The Derryn Hinch Justice Party and the Online Direct Democracy candidates expressed ambivalence while the Sex Party was sympathetic to Palestinian rights but did not sign APAN's pledge.
- Candidates from the right-wing Liberty Alliance, Christian Democratic Party, and Family First opposed Palestinian rights and expressed support for Israel using Christian Zionist arguments.

These findings show that APAN has conducted research to identify candidates and political parties who were sympathetic to the Palestinians, ambivalent, or hostile. APAN would then target pro-Palestinian parties and candidates such as the Australian Greens, Socialist Alliance, and pro-Palestinian Labor MPs like Parke and Vamvakinou for leveraging and coalition building activities while avoiding hostile pro-Israel parties like the Liberty Alliance, CDP, and Family First.

Targeting

This research found that APAN targeted these sympathetic segments by allocating resources and products (such as fundraising dinners, public meetings, sympathetic press releases, and social media posts) to reaching them:

1. APAN released a statement by Liberal MP Laundy praising APAN's advocacy work at their 2014 annual dinner (Laundy, 2014).
2. President Browning and Executive member Peter Slezak have defended Labor MP Parke's endorsement of BDS movement against criticism by the ECAJ (Slezak & Browning, 2014).
3. APAN (2014k, 2016l) has praised Labor MPs Hall, Hart, and Zappia, and Senator Urquhart for advocating the recognition of Palestinian statehood and condemning the Israeli military's detention of Palestinian children.
4. APAN (2015g, 2015h) has praised the Australian Greens for adopting a policy recognising Palestinian statehood in November 2015.
5. Reflecting the warm relationship between APAN and the Greens, Senator Rhiannon and MP Adam Bandt have participated at APAN events including its 2014 annual dinner and the 2016 Melbourne Candidates Forum (APAN, 2014h, 2016m).
6. APAN (2016l) has praised Nick Xenophon Team (NXT) leader Nick Xenophon and MP Rebecca Sharkie for condemning Israeli

settlements and calling for the Australian Government to pressure Israel to reform their juvenile military court system.
7. Hosting sympathetic Australian parliamentarians including NPA MP Coulton, Greens leader Natale, Greens Senator Janet Rice, and Labor MP Vamvakinou as speakers and guests of honour at their 2017 annual dinner (APAN, 2017e).

These interactions show that APAN has sought to target sympathetic politicians by issuing public statements and social media posts praising their support for the Palestinians. In addition, APAN has allocated resources to co-opting them into their advocacy work by featuring them as guests at their fundraising meetings and public speaking functions. While the Green and Labor politicians were most receptive to APAN's outreaches and advocacy work, the presence of Coalition and NXT politicians reflects APAN's desire to build cross-party support for changing Australian foreign policy towards Israel-Palestine.

Positioning

A content analysis of APAN's communications output (including webpages, press releases, social media posts, and op-ed columns) found that the organisation practised "psychological positioning" to promote the Palestinian cause in Australia. Whereas "real positioning" seeks to alter the product to cater for the market, psychological positioning focuses on altering perceptions of their product (Bartle & Griffiths, 2002). The Network's messages and arguments can be organised into four major themes and narratives:

1. **The Israeli-Palestine conflict is a "David versus Goliath" struggle in which the Palestinians are fighting for freedom and self-determination**. APAN has framed Palestinian actions such as the "Knife Intifada" as a response to Israeli "provocations" such as restrictions on Palestinian access to the Temple Mount (Harem al-Sharif) and Jerusalem's Old City, home demolitions, settlement expansion, and alleged extra-judicial killings (Shaik & Morrison, 2015). In addition, APAN (2014a, 2016k) has worked with allies such as the Australian journalist John Lyons and Australian politicians to raise awareness of the Israeli military's detention of Palestinian children. APAN (2018b, 2018h) has also highlighted

the imprisonment of Palestinian activist Ahed Tamimi and likened Palestinian resistance to the Black Lives Movement (BLM). The "David versus Goliath" narrative has also been promoted by senior Palestinian figures including Palestinian Executive Member Hanan Ashrawi and former Palestinian Prime Minister Dr Salam Fayyad (APAN, 2015a, 2015e), showing that APAN supports Palestinian public diplomacy and advocacy efforts. APAN also endorses a "win-win solution" to the Israel-Palestine conflict where a "just and prosperous" Palestine can live beside Israel (APAN, 2015j).

2. **Israel is committing human rights abuses and aggression against the Palestinians**. APAN has highlighted alleged Israeli human rights abuses including the 2015 Duma arson attack, a 2016 public opinion survey claiming that half of Israeli Jews objected to Arabs teaching their children, and claiming that the 2018 Nation State Law promoted "Apartheid" between Jews and Arabs (APAN 2015b, 2016e, 2018d). APAN (2012c, 2014f, 2018f) has also condemned Israeli military actions during the 2012 Gaza conflict, 2014 Gaza conflict, and the 2018 Gaza March of Return, accusing Israel of targeting non-combatants and violating international law. APAN's President Browning (2015c) has also condemned the Israeli occupation of Palestinian Territories for violating international law and displacing Palestinians. In addition, APAN (2017c, 2018f) has called on Israel to end its occupation of the West Bank and blockade of Gaza, which are key Palestinian goals and demands.

3. **Australia needs to speak up for Palestinian rights and statehood and hold Israel accountable for human rights abuses**. APAN (2012a) has urged the Australian Government to hold Israel accountable for human rights abuses such as the Gaza Blockade, settlement expansion, and administrative detention. APAN (2012a) has also called for Australia to unilaterally recognise Palestinian statehood and support multilateral peace negotiations between Israel and the Palestinians, claiming that bilateral peace negotiations are untenable due to the asymmetry between Israel and the Palestinians. To appeal to an Australian audience, APAN (2015j) claims that Australia's unquestioned support for Israel despite its alleged human rights violations goes against the Australian values of fairness and justice.

4. **Anti-Semitism is real but should not be used to silence legitimate criticism of Israeli crimes against the Palestinians and Zionism**. APAN has defended the BDS movement against allega-

tions of anti-Semitism, claiming that the transnational advocacy network is only interested in advancing Palestinian rights, self-determination, and holding Israel accountable for human rights violations (APAN, 2013e). In response to Liberal MP Michael Sukkar's speech denouncing BDS as an anti-Semitic "hate movement," Browning countered that BDS was targeting companies profiting from Israeli settlement expansion and Palestinian home demolitions (APAN, 2016b).

Based on these four arguments and narratives, APAN's positioning strategies consist of presenting the Palestinians as fighting for freedom and self-determination against Israeli "settler-colonialism" and calling on Australia to speak up for Palestinian rights and criticise Israel for its perceived wrongdoings. APAN also opposes anti-Semitism as part of its opposition to racism and bigotry in general. However, the Network argues that individuals and movements such as the BDS campaign seeking to hold Israel accountable for its treatment of the Palestinians are not motivated by anti-Semitic hatred but rather a desire to advance Palestinian human rights and self-determination. In short, APAN seeks to convince their Australian audience that the Palestinians are the "David" and that Israel is the "Goliath." APAN's pro-Palestinian messages and arguments show that the Network sees itself as working as part of a global Palestinian solidarity network to advance Palestinian rights and aspirations.

Analysis

APAN has fulfilled all three stages of the STP process. First, APAN has segmented the political market for the purpose of identifying sympathetic individuals and parties who can be targeted for coalition building and lobbying. Unlike other groups, APAN does not appear to have adapted its marketing to meet the needs and expectations of different markets since politicians appear to be the main target of its segmentation activities. Second, APAN has targeted these sympathetic elements by strategically allocating resources such as its communications output and relational activities to reaching political allies. This fits in with APAN's long-term goal of changing Australian foreign policy and political discourse in favour of the Palestinians. Third, APAN has conducted psychological positioning by framing the Israel-Palestine conflict as a "David versus Goliath" struggle revolving around Palestinian resistance to Israel settler-colonialism. APAN argues that Australia should help advance Palestinian rights and address Israeli wrongdoings. Despite these useful findings, this research generated little information about APAN's segmentation and targeting activities towards civil society groups and activists.

Internal Marketing

According to APAN's Constitution and its membership application form, membership is open to individuals and organisations that share its mission and objectives: namely to advocate for an end to the Israel-Palestine conflict, promote peace within the framework of UN resolutions and international law, build the capacity of like-minded organisations in Australia, and foster alliances between like-minded organisations in Australia and the international community. APAN (n.d.-c, n.d.-d, 2016i) also has separate membership packages for individuals and organisations that include membership fees. Larger organisations (groups with 5000 members and above) have higher membership fees and voting rights than smaller groups and individuals, suggesting that organisations with a bigger clout have more influence in APAN's decision-making process. The content analysis suggests that APAN pursues a base strategy since it limits membership to individuals and groups that share its objectives of advancing Palestinian rights and self-determination. These preliminary observations were also supported by its Vimeo promotional video and a webpage promoting their 2015 annual dinner, which emphasised APAN's commitment to advancing Palestinian rights and self-determination by working with like-minded groups and influencing political, public, and media discourses on Palestine (APAN, 2015f, 2018i).

The content analysis was corroborated by Morrison (personal communication, April 7, 2020), who explained that APAN encouraged its members to help advance its aims and goals through petition campaigns, protests, vigils, and educational events. When asked about how APAN promoted a sense of loyalty and purpose among its members and supporters, Morrison said that people were attracted to APAN by their passion for Palestinian human rights and justice. She also clarified that APAN did not seek to promote a sense of loyalty to their group but wanted them to be able to advocate for a more "just world." Together, the content analysis and the interview confirmed that APAN has pursued a base strategy by relying on purposive incentives to promote a product that resonates with its core supporters: advancing Palestinian rights and statehood. Quoting Pettitt (2015, p. 147), "activist commitment to this product remains strong as long as the product does not deviate from these goals and cause."

Analysis

The content analysis and interview with Morrison showed that APAN has pursued a base strategy by using its commitment to advancing Palestinian rights and self-determination to attract members and supporters who share these goals. APAN has advanced these goals and cause by using a range of relational activities to promote these goals.

PUBLIC DIPLOMACY AND NATION BRANDING

APAN has supported Palestinian public diplomacy and nation branding by networking with Palestinian officials and diplomats, producing pro-Palestinian informational content, and sponsoring guest speaking events and informational trips to the Palestinian Territories. These communicational output and relational activities seek to manage the Palestinians' public image in Australia and raise awareness of the Palestinian cause.

First, APAN has cultivated relations and networked with Palestinian officials and diplomats while leveraging on its access to sympathetic Australian politicians:

- A natural ally is the Palestinian "General Delegation to Australia, New Zealand and the Pacific," the de facto representative of the Palestinian Authority in Australasia. APAN (2014i, 2014e, 2016h) has cultivated a friendly relationship with the Palestinian Ambassador Izzat Salah Abdulhadi, whom they hosted at their 2014 and 2016 annual dinners. APAN (2013b) also worked with the Palestinian Delegation to host Palestinian doctor Mona El-Farra during her guest speaking tour of Australia.
- Publicising former Palestinian Prime Minister Salam Fayyad's 2015 address to the Australian Press Club (APAN, 2015e).
- During the 2015 ALP National Conference, APAN (2015a) and the Australian Jewish Democratic Society (AJDS) hosted a video presentation by Palestinian Executive Committee member Dr Hanan Ashrawi.
- APAN has also worked with the Australian Parliamentary Friends of Palestine and Australian Parliamentary UN Friendship group to host visiting speakers and promote the 2014 UN Year of Solidarity at the Australian Parliament (APAN, 2012a, 2014d).

These interactions show that APAN has gained access to some Palestinian officials and diplomats, most notably Ambassador Abdulhadi and Ashrawi. APAN has supported Palestinian public diplomacy efforts by hosting Palestinian guest speakers. The Network also works with sympathetic Australian parliamentarians to raise awareness of the Palestinian cause at the Australian Parliament.

Second, APAN has used its communications output (including press releases, social media posts, and op-ed commentary) to support Palestinian public diplomacy and nation branding with the goal of promoting awareness and sympathy for the Palestinian cause in Australia including:

- In terms of media management, APAN has published pro-Palestinian op-ed columns and letters in several Australian and international newspapers and media platforms including *The Age, The Australian,* the *Canberra Times,* the *Courier-Mail, The Guardian,* the Jewish news website J-Wire, *Labour Herald, Melbourne Anglican,* and the *Sydney Morning Herald* (Browning, 2014, 2015a, 2015b, 2017a, 2017b; Browning & Barak, 2018; Dally, 2018; Slezak & Browning, 2014; Slezak, 2012).
- In addition, APAN members have participated in media interviews and reports with several Australian news broadcasters including 3CR Community Radio, the Australian Broadcasting Corporation (ABC), the Special Broadcasting Service (SBS), and *The Wire* (Bartlett, 2015; Carisbrooke, 2014; Oriti, 2017; Sferruzzi, 2015). APAN member Slezak also participated in an ABC radio documentary entitled *Breaking the Silence* which featured dissident Israelis, Palestinians, and human rights activities. This documentary portrayed the Palestinians as a resilient, courteous, and hospitable people enduring a "brutal" Israeli military occupation, thus advancing the "David versus Goliath" narrative (Melville, 2012).
- On the social media front, APAN (2013a, 2013f, 2013g, 2014b, 2014j, 2017d, 2017g) has used its Twitter account to highlight Palestinian-related issues including Palestinian United Nations membership status, Israeli settlement expansion, the Israeli military occupation, the detention of Palestinian children, the plight of Negev Bedouins facing eviction, PayPal's discriminatory practices against Palestinians, and alleged anti-Palestinian racism by senior Israeli policy-makers.

In support of Palestinian public diplomacy and nation branding, APAN has submitted pro-Israel op-ed columns and letters to major Australian media outlets while also taking part in media interviews, news reports, and documentaries. In addition, APAN has also highlighted Palestinian-related stories and issues on its Twitter account. Taken together, APAN's communicational output presents the Israel-Palestine conflict as a David versus Goliath struggle where the Palestinians are fighting for human rights, justice, and self-determination.

Third, APAN has conducted various relational activities including information trips to Israel and the Palestinian Territories, guest speaking engagements, fundraising dinners, and even sponsoring a Palestinian cultural centre to promote Palestinian public diplomacy and nation branding in Australia. APAN's study tours are a key pillar of its relational image management activities. Their study tours are working tours, usually between 8 and 12 participants, which involve meeting Palestinian peoples in the Palestinian Territories, Israel, Lebanon, and Jordan, and visiting their homes and communities. The tour programme costs AU$7000 and includes international economy-class airfare, in-country accommodation and transportation, meals, a pre-departure briefing, an information booklet and prescribed reading list, and access to experts on Palestine (APAN n.d.-e). These study tours usually involved meeting with Palestinian refugees in Lebanon and visiting Jerusalem and West Bank cities including Ramallah and Bethlehem. Besides meeting with Palestinian and Israeli officials, sympathetic local Palestinian and Israeli civil society groups including the Palestinian Women's Humanitarian Organisation and the Israeli Committee Against House Demolitions, the study tours also include meeting with the Australian Representative Office in Ramallah to learn about Australian aid projects. APAN's study tour coordinator is Lisa Arnold, a humanitarian aid worker who had previously worked for APHEDA, the aid agency of the Australian Council of Trade Unions (ACTU) (Bartlett, 2015). The study tours are open to anyone interested in Palestine and the Palestinians with past participants having included politicians, journalists, and trade unionists (APAN, 2017b, 2018g; Robin, 2016). Besides educating Australians about the plight of Palestinians, APAN's study tours also seek to build relations with sympathetic Palestinian and Israeli individuals and groups. APAN has particularly targeted influential policy-makers, media, and civil society leaders with the goal of shifting the political and public discourses on Israel-Palestine.

APAN also has hosted several guest speaking functions and a Palestinian information centre:

- APAN's guest speaking engagements have featured several Palestinian and international allies including Israeli historian Ilan Pappe, Palestinian doctor Mona El-Farra, Israeli peace activist Jeff Halper, United Nations Special Rapporteur Richard Falk, former Palestinian Prime Minister Salam Fayyad, Palestinian activists Rafeef Ziadah, Ali Abunimah, and Ramzy Baroud, Israeli journalist Gideon Levy, and British musician and activist Roger Waters (APAN, 2012b, 2013d, 2015d, 2016c, 2017f, 2018c, 2018e; Morrison, 2013).
- Publicising the allied Australian Friends of Palestine Association's (AFOPA) new "Palestinian Centre" in Adelaide selling both informational resources and Palestinian fair-trade products (APAN, 2016a). Besides informing Adelaide residents about the Palestinian people, this shop helps Palestinian communities to sell their produce at a sustainable level.

In short, these speaking engagements and fair-trade shops not only help to get the message out but enable sympathetic Australians to build ties with Palestinians and aid Palestinian businesses and producers.

Analysis

APAN has engaged in informal public diplomacy and nation branding in support of the Palestinians through its communicational output and relational activities. First, the Network has cultivated relationships with several Palestinian diplomats and officials (most notably Palestinian Ambassador Abdulhadi, former Prime Minister Fayyad, and Executive Committee member Ashrawi) while networking with sympathetic Australian parliamentarians. Second, APAN has produced various online, print, and audiovisual communications output presenting the Palestinian narrative to the Australian media and public.

Third, APAN has sponsored various relational activities including information trips to the Palestinian Territories, guest speaking engagements featuring Palestinian and international activists, and promoting a Palestinian information centre in coordination with another Palestinian solidarity group. Due to the asymmetrical situation facing the Palestinians, APAN has focused on promoting Palestinian rights and self-determination and combating negative imagery and perceptions. While the Network has promoted Palestinian culture and heritage through its information tours and information centre, these took second place to advocacy and image management.

Conclusion

This chapter analysed the communications and advocacy activities of the Australia Palestine Advocacy Network against the researcher's political marketing and public diplomacy framework. APAN met most of the criteria of this framework. In terms of marketing orientation, APAN has followed the four stages of a product-oriented group. First, APAN has a clear product which it is unwilling to compromise on. Second, the Network has used its communications output including its website, newsletters, and media op-ed commentary to promote its product. Third, APAN's campaigning has taken the form of networking with like-minded allies and lobbying influential Australian stakeholders. Finally, APAN has used its communications output to communicate its achievements and successes.

APAN has also followed all three stages of the STP process. First, APAN has segmented Australian political parties and politicians to identify those who are most sympathetic to Palestinian human rights and justice. Though Morrison stated that APAN did not conduct segmentation, the author's research found that the organisation segmented sympathetic politicians. Second, APAN has targeted sympathetic politicians and parties through various relational activities including speaking engagements, fundraising dinners, and study tours. These activities show that APAN has allocated resources and products where there is a market for them and when it helps them achieve their goals. Third, APAN has conducted psychological positioning by framing the Israel-Palestine conflict as a "David versus Goliath" conflict where the Palestinians are fighting for human rights and self-determination against Israeli "settler-colonialism."

In terms of internal marketing, the content analysis and Morrison's interview showed that APAN has pursued a base strategy by appealing to its members and supporters' desire to advance Palestinian rights and self-determination through its relational activities including mass gatherings and advocacy work.

Finally, APAN has supported Palestinian public diplomacy and nation branding on both a formal and informal level. Formal contacts have included networking with Palestinian officials and diplomats including

Ambassador Abdulhadi, former Prime Minister Fayyad, and Executive Committee member Ashrawi. Informal public diplomacy and nation branding has taken the form of publishing pro-Palestinian informational output, hosting guest speaking engagements, and organising informational trips to the Palestinian Territories. Several of these activities are done in coordination with other Palestinian and allied activists and groups in Australia and abroad.

References

APAN. (2011a, May 24). *Media Release: Launch of Australia Palestine Advocacy Network.* https://apanaustralia.files.wordpress.com/2011/10/media-release-110524.pdf

APAN. (2011b, November 21). *Palestine in Australian politics 2011.* https://apan.org.au/2011/11/19/palestine-in-australian-politics-2011/

APAN. (2012a, June). *APAN presses Canberra for policy shift.* https://apan.org.au/apan-activities/apan-presses-canberra-for-policy-shift/

APAN. (2012b, September 19). *APAN hosts Prof Ilan Pappe at the National Press Club.* https://apan.org.au/apan-activities/apan-hosts-prof-ilan-pappe-at-the-national-press-club/

APAN. (2012c, November 15). *Media Release: Israeli [sic] must be condemned for its attacks on Gaza.* https://apan.org.au/media-releases/media-release-15-nov-2012/

APAN. (2012d, December 20). *Palestine in Australian politics 2012.* https://apan.org.au/2012/12/20/palestine-in-australian-politics-2012/

APAN [@APAN4Palestine]. (2013a, June 26). *Please sign AVAAZ petition to stand with Negev Bedouins who are at risk of being forced off their land.* https://twitter.com/APAN4Palestine/status/349685719100428288

APAN. (2013b, August). *Candidate responses prior to 2013 federal election.* https://apan.org.au/party-positions-on-the-question-of-palestine/candidate-responses/

APAN. (2013c, September). *Party positions on the question of Palestine.* https://apan.org.au/party-positions-on-the-question-of-palestine/

APAN [@APAN4Palestine]. (2013d, September 2). *Two amazing speakers in Oz this month - Israeli ProfJeff Halper AND UN Special Rapporteur Richard Falk details.* https://twitter.com/APAN4Palestine/status/374416046188277761

APAN [@APAN4Palestine]. (2013e, November 13). *Prof Peter Slezak asks "Is it anti-Semitic to protest injustice".* https://twitter.com/APAN4Palestine/status/400498939910045696

APAN [@APAN4Palestine]. (2013f, November 26). *Australia's U-turn on Israeli settlements in occupied territories is shameful @MichaelBrull.* https://twitter.com/APAN4Palestine/status/405159312491687936

APAN. (2013g, December 22). *Palestine in Australian politics 2013.* https://apan.org.au/2013/12/22/palestine-in-australian-politics-2013/
APAN. (2014a, February 11). *Media Release: STONE COLD JUSTICE (ABC/The Australian) welcomed by APAN.* https://apan.org.au/media-releases/media-release-11-feb-2014/
APAN [@APAN4Palestine]. (2014b, February 11). *APAN MR applaudes [sic] @australian & @4corners for STONE COLD JUSTICE.* https://twitter.com/APAN4Palestine/status/433028025735585792
APAN [@APAN4Palestine]. (2014c, March 6). *Leaving after 50 mtgs this wk! Gr8 to have Pollies on all sides supporting #Palestine & just peace 4 all #auspol.* https://twitter.com/APAN4Palestine/status/441468530131611648
APAN. (2014d, March 24). *Parliament honors UN Year of Solidarity.* https://apan.org.au/apan-activities/federal_parl_un_yr_event/
APAN [@APAN4Palestine]. (2014e, June 26). *APAN Fundraising Dinner in Sydney on 29th August. HE Izzat Abdulhadi as Guest Speaker. Visit our website for invite.* https://twitter.com/APAN4Palestine/status/482042127803617280
APAN. (2014f, July 22). *Media Release: Stop the Fighting, Lift the Siege.* https://apan.org.au/media-releases/media-release-22-july-2014/
APAN. (2014g, July 27). *Palestine in Australian politics 2014 (January–June).* https://apan.org.au/2014/07/27/palestine-in-australian-politics-2014-january-june/
APAN. (2014h, August 29). *APAN Dinner – honoring the UN International Year of Solidarity.* https://apan.org.au/apan-activities/apan-dinner-honoring-the-un-international-year-of-solidarity/
APAN [@APAN4Palestine]. (2014i, September 30). *#Palestine envoy urges Australian politicians to play a positive role for peace by visiting Palestine.* https://twitter.com/APAN4Palestine/status/516674768863789057
APAN [@APAN4Palestine]. (2014j, October 15). *British MPs vote overwhelmingly (274–12) to recognise a #PalestinianState.* https://twitter.com/APAN4Palestine/status/522125205154439168
APAN. (2014k, December). *C'mon Australia: Vote to end the Occupation, Recognise Palestine!.* https://apan.good.do/vote-yes/pages/recognition-of-palestine/
APAN. (2014l, December 3). *Palestine in Australian politics 2014 (July–December).* https://apan.org.au/2014/11/23/palestine-in-australian-politics-2014-july-december/
APAN. (2015a, July 29). *Dr Ashrawi at ALP National Conference.* Vimeo. https://vimeo.com/134901286
APAN [@APAN4Palestine]. (2015b, August 10). *Father of Palestinian Toddler killed in West Bank Arson attack dies in Hospital.* https://twitter.com/APAN4Palestine/status/630524670907777024

APAN. (2015c, August 23). *Palestine in Australian politics 2015 (January–June)*. https://apan.org.au/2015/08/23/palestine-in-australian-politics-2015-january-june/

APAN. (2015d, September). *Dr Salam Fayyad visit to Australia*. https://apan.org.au/apan-activities/dr-salam-fayyad-visit-to-australia/

APAN. (2015e, October 1). *Dr Fayyad at the National Press Club, Canberra*. Vimeo. https://vimeo.com/141013296

APAN. (2015f, October 30). *APAN Annual Dinner 2015*. https://apan.org.au/2015/10/30/apan-annual-dinner-2015/

APAN. (2015g, November 13). *Australian Greens recognise Palestine*. https://apan.org.au/2015/11/13/australian-greens-recognise-palestine/

APAN [@APAN4Palestine]. (2015h, November 13). *@APAN4Palestine welcomes Australian @Greens resolution to recognise #Palestine*. https://twitter.com/APAN4Palestine/status/664983864021024768

APAN. (2015i, December 1). *Palestine in Australian politics 2015 (July–December)*. https://apan.org.au/2015/11/24/palestine-in-australian-politics-2015-july-december/

APAN. (2015j, December 23). *APAN Christmas message*. https://apan.org.au/2015/12/23/apan-christmas-message/

APAN. (2016a, February 4). *Adelaide opens Palestine Centre*. https://apan.org.au/2016/02/04/adelaide-opens-palestinian-center-for-peace/

APAN. (2016b, March 7). *Bishop Browning responds to speech by Michael Sukkar MP*. https://apan.org.au/2016/03/07/bishop-browning-responds-to-speech-by-michael-sukkar-mp/

APAN [@APAN4Palestine]. (2016c, March 23). *Two amazing Palestinians are in Australia - @RafeefZiadah and @AliAbunimah - have you booked to see them?*. https://twitter.com/APAN4Palestine/status/712400516089835521

APAN. (2016d, May 5). *Palestine in Australian politics 2016 (January–June)*. https://apan.org.au/2016/01/01/palestine-in-australian-politics-2016-january-june/

APAN [@APAN4Palestine]. (2016e, June 1). *Almost 1/2 Israeli Jews don't want Arabs teaching their kids! @Jerusalem_Post says burgeoning racism in Israel*. https://twitter.com/APAN4Palestine/status/737831896931926016

APAN. (2016f, June 23). *Overview of candidate responses to I Vote Palestine campaign*. https://apan.org.au/2016/06/23/overview-of-candidate-responses-to-i-vote-palestine-campaign/

APAN. (2016g, June 30). *What did the candidates say?*. https://apan.org.au/2016/06/30/what-did-the-candidates-say/

APAN. (2016h, August 15). *APAN Annual Dinner – 24 September*. https://apan.org.au/2016/08/15/apan-annual-dinner-24-september/

APAN. (2016i, September). *Australia Palestine Advocacy Network Incorporated Constitution*. https://apanaustralia.files.wordpress.com/2018/05/constitution_sept_2016.pdf

APAN. (2016j, October 13). *Palestine in Australian politics 2016 (July-Dec)*. https://apan.org.au/2016/07/20/palestine-in-australian-politics-2016-july-dec/

APAN. (2016k, November 28). *Parliamentarians in unity to stop the abuse of Palestinian children*. https://apan.org.au/2016/11/28/parliamentarians-in-unity-to-stop-the-abuse-of-palestinian-children/

APAN. (2016l, November 29). *Parliamentarians call for Israel to stop ill-treatment of Palestinian children by their military*. https://apan.org.au/2016/11/22/nwttac/

APAN. (2016m, June). *Melbourne Candidates Forum – highlight*. Vimeo. https://vimeo.com/173008926

APAN. (2017a, February). *Candidate responses*. https://apan.org.au/candidate-responses/

APAN [@APAN4Palestine]. (2017b, April 5). *Our study tour with @Greens began today with Knesset mtgs. MK Tamar Zanberg- "advocating to end the occupation most pro-Israel thing"*. https://twitter.com/APAN4Palestine/status/849590780079595521

APAN. (2017c, June 4). *Media Release: 50 years of Israeli military occupation of Palestine*. https://apan.org.au/50-years-of-israeli-military-occupation-of-palestine/

APAN [@APAN4Palestine]. (2017d, July 4). *Paypal - stop discriminating against Palestinians - Sign the Petition! #Paypal4palestine*. https://twitter.com/APAN4Palestine/status/882092307067031552

APAN [@APAN4Palestine]. (2017e, August 10). *Our dinner features @MarkCoultonMP @RichardDiNatale & @janet_rice @MariaVamvakinou @SharanBurrow (vid) @TasChop TIX*. https://twitter.com/APAN4Palestine/status/895404333369610250

APAN [@APAN4Palestine]. (2017f, November 25). *Excited to be with @gideonle for his first public Aussie event. More events at http://apan.org.au #esml #palestinesymposium @AFOPA_Australia*. https://twitter.com/APAN4Palestine/status/934320853046591488

APAN [@APAN4Palestine]. (2017g, December 4). *Incitement Report for November 2017: Examples of recent inflammatory comments and incitement by Israeli officials and leaders*. https://twitter.com/APAN4Palestine/status/937481188515516416

APAN. (2018a, January 1). *Palestine in Australian politics 2017*. https://apan.org.au/2018/01/01/palestine-in-australian-politics-2017/

APAN [@APAN4Palestine]. (2018b, January 30). *How #Israel created a #Palestinian heroine #FreeAhed.* https://twitter.com/APAN4Palestine/status/958124381745553408

APAN. (2018c, February 3). *BOOK NOW: Roger Waters on Palestine.* https://apan.org.au/2018/02/03/book-now-roger-waters-in-conversation-on-palestine/

APAN [@APAN4Palestine]. (2018d, February 21). *#Israel's Justice Minister endorses apartheid -- the #Jewish state 'at the expense of #equality'.* https://twitter.com/APAN4Palestine/status/966465669779750912

APAN [@APAN4Palestine]. (2018e, May 14). *@jennineak Dr @RamzyBaroud speaking at #Nakba70 commemoration events...* https://twitter.com/APAN4Palestine/status/995909091280076800

APAN. (2018f, May 22). *The Australian Government Appears Determined to Cover Israel's Crimes.* https://apan.org.au/2018/05/22/apan-condemns-australia-rejecting-unhrc-resolution/

APAN. (2018g, May 31). *Palestine in Australian politics 2018.* https://apan.org.au/2018/03/07/palestine-in-australian-politics-2018/

APAN. (2018h, July 21). *Noura Erakat: Palestine Futures, full talk and Q&A.* Vimeo. https://vimeo.com/281037312

APAN. (2018i, August 16). *Australia Palestine Advocacy Network.* Vimeo. https://vimeo.com/285390443

APAN. (n.d.-a). *About.* Retrieved September 22, 2019, from https://apan.org.au/about/

APAN. (n.d.-b). *APAN people.* Retrieved September 22, 2019, from https://apan.org.au/people/

APAN. (n.d.-c). *Join Us!.* Retrieved September 22, 2019, from https://crm.apan.org.au/memberships/

APAN. (n.d.-d). *Membership form.* Retrieved March 17, 2020, from https://crm.apan.org.au/wp-content/uploads/civicrm/persist/contribute/files/membership_form_updated.docx

APAN. (n.d.-e). *Tours to Palestine.* Retrieved September 24, 2019, from https://apan.org.au/study_tour/

Bartle, J. & Griffiths, D. (2002). Social-Psychological, Economic and Marketing Models of Voting Behaviour Compared. In N.J. O'Shaughnessy & S.C.M. Henneberg, The Idea of Political Marketing (pp. 19–37). Praeger.

Bartlett, J. (2015, October 13). *APAN Study Tour and the reasons for going.* [Audio podcast] 3CR Community Radio. https://www.3cr.org.au/hometime-tuesday/episode-201510131600/us-japan-bendigo

Browning, G. (2014, April 9). *Abbas's move to sign global treaties shows Kerry's peace bid has failed.* APAN. https://apan.org.au/apan-in-the-news/april2014oped/

Browning, G. (2015a, May). Getting the facts right on Palestine. *The Melbourne Anglican*, (536), https://apanaustralia.files.wordpress.com/2011/09/getting-the-facts-right-on-palestine_bp-george-browning.pdf

Browning, G. (2015b, July 22). George Browning has this to say about the lingering Israeli-Palestine conflict. *Labour Herald*. http://web.archive.org/web/20151029214617/https://www.laborherald.com.au/economy/george-browning-has-this-to-say-about-the-lingering-israeli-palestine-conflict/

Browning, G. (2017a, January 4). Malcolm Turnbull is wrong. Australia should not side with Israel. *Courier Mail*. http://web.b.ebscohost.com.ezproxy.auckland.ac.nz/ehost/detail/detail?vid=5&sid=1419bc5d-869e-4b41-820b-a0c07f1fa56d%40pdc-v-sessmgr05&bdata=JnNpdGU9ZWhvc3QtbGl2ZSZzY29wZT1zaXRl#AN=9X9CMLNEWSMMGLSTRY000203472426&db=anh

Browning, G. (2017b, February 22). Turnbull has clearly chosen: Australia stands alone on Israel. *The Guardian*. https://www.theguardian.com/commentisfree/2017/feb/22/turnbull-has-clearly-chosen-to-side-with-netanyahu-australia-stands-alone-on-israel

Browning, G., & Barak, S. (2018, May 13). Palestinians undefeated as Israel celebrates 70th anniversary. *Sydney Morning Herald*. https://www.smh.com.au/world/middle-east/palestinians-undefeated-as-israel-celebrates-70th-anniversary-20180511-p4zeut.html

Carisbrooke, P. (2014, April 24). Palestinians plans to form unity government. *SBS News*. https://www.sbs.com.au/news/palestinians-plan-to-form-unity-government

Dally, B. (2018, May 19). Great March for Palestinian Return. *The Australian*. https://search-proquest-com.ezproxy.auckland.ac.nz/docview/2040827062/9ECFFE32EA3945A4PQ/4?accountid=8424

Laundy, C. (2014, August 29). *Message from Craig Laundy MP, Member for Reid and Co-Chair of the Federal Parliamentary Friends of Palestine Group*. APAN. https://apanaustralia.files.wordpress.com/2014/09/29-08-14-apan-dinner-message_laundy.pdf

Lees-Marshment, J. (2004). *The political marketing revolution: Transforming the government of the UK*. Manchester University Press.

Melville, K. (Host). (2012, September 9). Breaking the Silence. In *360documentaries*. ABC Radio National. https://www.abc.net.au/radionational/programs/360/new-document/4240142

Morrison, J. (2013, May 28). *Media Release: Visiting Doctor from Gaza asks parliamentarians for urgent action*. APAN. https://apan.org.au/media-releases/media-release-28-may-2013/

Oriti, T. (Host). (2017, December 6). Fears of violence as US recognises Jerusalem as Israel's capital. In *PM*. ABC News. https://www.abc.net.au/radio/programs/pm/us-recognises-jerusalem-as-israels-capital/9233334

Parke, M. (2013, September). *The Hon Melissa Parke MP, Labor Member for Fremantle*. APAN. https://apan.org.au/party-positions-on-the-question-of-palestine/the-hon-melissa-parke-mp-labor-member-for-fremantle/

Pettitt, R. T. (2015). Internal part political relationship marketing: Encouraging activism amongst local party members. In J. Lees-Marshment (Ed.), *Routledge handbook of political marketing* (pp. 137–150). Routledge.

Robin, M. (2016, December 22). *Palestinian lobby joins the junket game*. Crikey. https://www.crikey.com.au/2016/12/22/palestinian-lobby-joins-the-junket-game/

Sferruzzi, J. (Producer). (2015, March 18). Israeli elections See Netanyahu returned [audio podcast]. *The Wire*. http://thewire.org.au/story/israeli-elections-see-netanyahu-returned/

Shaik, M. (2015, October 26). *Media Release 26 October 2015: APAN Statement on BDS*. APAN. https://apan.org.au/media-releases/media-release-26-october-2015/

Shaik, M. & Morrison, J. (2015, October 7). *Media Release: APAN Statement on the Violence in the Occupied Palestinian Territories*. APAN. https://apan.org.au/media-releases/media-release-7-october-2015/

Slezak, P. (2012, May 31). Invitation cancelled. *J-Wire*. http://web.archive.org/web/20120606131752/http://www.jwire.com.au/news/invitation-reversed/25352

Slezak, P., & Browning, G. (2014, November 13). MP's courageous speech defies disgraceful descent into gutter. *Canberra Times*. http://web.archive.org/web/20141124095619/http://www.canberratimes.com.au/comment/ct-letters/bully-solution-exists-20141112-3k6z7.html

Storey, J. (2013, September). *John Storey, Greens candidate for Berowa*. APAN. https://apan.org.au/party-positions-on-the-question-of-palestine/john-storey-greens-candidate-for-berowa/

Stove, M. (2013, September). *Mr Michael Stove, Labor candidate for Berowra*. APAN. https://apan.org.au/party-positions-on-the-question-of-palestine/mr-michael-stove-labor-candidate-for-berowra/

CHAPTER 6

Conclusion

Abstract The conclusion outlines how this research addressed the question of how advocacy groups in New Zealand and Australia have used political marketing to support the public diplomacy and nation efforts of the Israeli and the Palestinian governments. It also considers whether the groups functioned as independent allies or proxies of state actors in terms of public diplomacy and nation branding. The chapter then discusses how the case studies met the various political marketing, public diplomacy, and nation branding criteria of the framework before reflecting on the value, strengths, and limitations of the author's synthesised analytical framework. The conclusion also outlines this study's contribution to the fields of advocacy, political marketing, public diplomacy, and nation branding. Finally, this chapter provides several lessons for practitioners in the areas of advocacy, political marketing, public diplomacy, and nation branding.

Keywords Marketing orientation • STP (segmentation, targeting, and positioning) • Internal marketing • Public diplomacy • Nation branding

Introduction

This book has explored the political marketing, public diplomacy, and nation branding activities of both pro-Israel and Palestinian solidarity groups in New Zealand and Australia. Throughout the course of the Israeli-Palestine conflict, the Israeli and Palestinian governments along with sympathetic non-state actors including advocacy groups have used public diplomacy, nation branding, and political marketing strategies and techniques to influence foreign public opinion, media coverage, and political elites. This struggle has reverberated through civil society, non-governmental organisations (NGOs), local government bodies, public institutions, trade unions, businesses, the news media, the Internet, and social media. In the process, both sides have constructed diametrically opposing narratives positing themselves as the victims and their opponents as the aggressors. While the Israeli Government and Zionist advocacy groups have framed Israel's struggle as a defensive one against anti-Semitism and Islamism, the Palestinian Authority and Palestinian solidarity groups including the Boycott, Divestment, and Sanctions (BDS) movement have framed the Palestinian struggle as an anti-colonial struggle against settler colonialism, Israeli military occupation, and "Apartheid." Besides exploring how political marketing can be used outside of party politics and elections by various actors, including advocacy groups, this research also investigates how non-state actors can contribute to public diplomacy and nation branding.

The Research

To begin addressing this issue, firstly, a multi-field literature review of advocacy, public diplomacy, nation branding, and political marketing was completed, including the literature relating to Israeli and Palestinian advocacy groups in New Zealand and Australia. This process identified four major gaps in existing academic literature including the limited attention to advocacy groups working on Israel-Palestine issues in New Zealand; the limited exploration of the advocacy group's political marketing, public diplomacy, and nation branding activities; the limited attention to Australian Palestinian solidarity groups and the limited exploration of Palestinian political marketing, public diplomacy, and nation branding.

However, the review also identified key concepts in existing work that could be adapted to suit the research focus, including advocacy work by

Keck and Sikkink (1998), Lang and Lang (1983), and Cobb and Elder (1972); political marketing work by Lees-Marshment (2004, 2014), Bartle and Griffiths (2002), and Pettitt (2015); public diplomacy work by Cull (2009), Gilboa (2001, 2008), and Zaharna (2009); and nation branding work by Szondi (2008), Beirman (2000, 2002), Brin (2006), Avraham (2009), Campo and Alvarez (2014).

Building on core concepts from these works, a new theoretical framework was created which combined advocacy, public diplomacy, nation branding, and political marketing research: A model of how advocacy groups can use political marketing to support the public diplomacy and nation branding efforts of the Israeli and the Palestinian governments. This argued that advocacy groups can incorporate political marketing, public diplomacy, and nation branding into their advocacy work:

- Marketing orientation: attracting new members through product, sales, and market-orientations.
- Segmentation, targeting, and positioning (STP): identifying sympathetic segments; targeting them through a range of activities; positioning their cause and messages in a way that would resonate with their target audience.
- Internal marketing: Mobilising members through a range of ideological, material, and democratic incentives.
- Public diplomacy and nation branding: Helping state actors and sub-national actors to manage their international image and advance their perceived national interests and aspirations by working with foreign officials, through their communications output and relational activities, cultural promotion, and image management.

Methodology

Empirical research was conducted to explore the extent to which advocacy groups were following this framework using a qualitative and comparative case studies approach. It analysed four groups: two pro-Israel groups and two Palestinian solidarity groups. The New Zealand case studies consisted of the Palestinian Solidarity Network Aotearoa (PSNA; formerly the New Zealand Palestine Solidarity Network, or NZPSN) and the Israel Institute of New Zealand (IINZ) while the Australian case studies consisted of the Australia/Israel & Jewish Affairs Council (AIJAC) and the Australia Palestine Advocacy Network (APAN). The research used several qualitative research methods including a content analysis of a range of web, social media, and print sources and qualitative interviews. Sources derived from the content analysis and interviews were analysed against the researcher's analytical framework using NVivo software.

A total of 1898 sources were analysed for the four case studies. These sources were supplemented by interviews with available practitioners from the four case studies: the PSNA's National Chair John Minto, the Israel Institute's Director David Cumin, and APAN's Executive Officer Jessica Morrison. Unfortunately, despite multiple attempts it was not possible to interview any current or former AIJAC staff members due to AIJAC's policy of not granting interviews, thus secondary sources were used to fill this gap in data. The data was analysed against the analytical framework using NVivo software.

RESEARCH QUESTION AND HYPOTHESIS

The author's research found that the four case studies used political marketing to support the public diplomacy and nation branding efforts of the Israeli and the Palestinian governments through various communicational output (such as websites, audio-visual media, and print media) and relational activities (such as public gatherings, fundraisers, and informational trips). To reiterate, they used a range of political marketing approaches and techniques including marketing orientations; segmentation, targeting, and positioning (STP); and internal marketing for the purposes of promoting their causes, identifying sympathetic segments, and mobilising supporters in New Zealand and Australia. They also supported the public diplomacy of these state actors by advancing their messages and interests through various online and print literature and media; lobbying and cultivating relationships with a range of political, media, and civil society actors; and organising various advocacy activities. The groups also conducted nation branding by promoting favourable images and countering negative imagery of the state or sub-national actor they were supporting through their communicational output and relational activities. In short, political marketing, public diplomacy, and nation branding permeated the groups' communicational output and advocacy activities.

This research supported the author's hypothesis that the groups functioned as independent allies who supported the public diplomacy and nation branding efforts of foreign state actors through their advocacy activities. The research did not support the null hypothesis that the groups were proxies created by foreign state actors to support their public diplomacy and nation branding activities. Despite their friendly interactions with foreign governments and their representatives, all four groups studied drew their leadership and support (including financial and material) from domestic support within Australia and New Zealand. While this research found that pro-Israel groups draw their support from local Jewish communities, Christian Zionists, and the political right, pro-Palestinian groups draw their support from the political left and the Arab and Muslim communities, suggesting that Israel-Palestine is becoming a polarising issue in left-right politics. The case for autonomy was also supported by the groups' varying levels of support and engagement with states' public diplomacy efforts. While the Zionist groups had more engagement with the Israeli Government and often followed the official Israeli narrative, the Palestinian solidarity groups tended to have less engagement with the Palestinian Authority and instead looked up to the BDS movement, a non-state transnational civil society actor, for leadership and guidance in carrying out their advocacy work and activities. This research found that the groups largely emerged in response to local conditions in Australia and New Zealand rather than through foreign interference in domestic affairs. AIJAC and the IINZ emerged in response to perceived anti-Israel sentiment in their countries, while APAN and the PSNA emerged to coordinate Palestinian solidarity activism nationally. Despite supporting states' public diplomacy efforts, these groups also sought to lobby and work with a range of domestic actors including political elites, the media, and other faith and ethnic communities. In short, these observations suggest that the advocacy groups should be classified as autonomous allies who supported the states' public diplomacy activities rather than as proxies of foreign state actors. The research findings and how they met the criteria of the research's political marketing, public diplomacy, and nation branding framework are outlined in the case studies' findings section below.

Case Studies' Findings

The four case studies met most of the criteria of the author's synthesised political marketing, public diplomacy, and nation branding framework. These findings are outlined in the paragraphs below and in Table 6.1.

Table 6.1 Did the advocacy groups adhere to the framework's criteria?

Groups	PSNA	IINZ	AIJAC	APAN
Marketing orientation				
Product-orientation	√			√
Sales-orientation		√	√	
Market-orientation				
Segmentation, targeting, and positioning (STP)				
Segmentation	√	√	√	√
Targeting	√	√	√	√
Positioning	√	√	√	√
Internal marketing				
Material incentives				
Base strategy	√	√	√	√
Empty vessel				
Dignified democracy				
Effective democracy				
Public diplomacy and nation branding				
Working with foreign officials		√	√	√
Producing literature and media	√	√	√	√
Cultural and heritage promotion	√	√	√	√
Crisis management	√	√	√	√
Public events and information trips	√	√	√	√

Marketing Orientation

Drawing upon Lees-Marshment's (2004) "product/sales/market-oriented framework," the author's research found that Palestinian solidarity groups tended to follow the characteristics of product-oriented advocacy groups, while pro-Israel groups tended to follow the characteristics of sales-oriented advocacy groups. The PSNA and APAN followed the four stages of product-oriented groups. First, they had a clear product (Palestinian rights and self-determination) which they were unwilling to compromise to meet public or elite opinion. Second, both groups have used their communications output including websites, social media accounts, newsletters, and op-ed commentary to promote their products. Third, the PSNA and APAN have campaigned for their cause through protests, public meetings, guest speaking engagements, networking with like-minded allies, and lobbying key stakeholders. Finally, both groups have used their communications output to promote their achievements and successes.

Both the Israel Institute and AIJAC followed the five stages of sales-oriented groups. First, they had a clear product (promoting Israel and Zionism and combating anti-Semitism) that they were unwilling to compromise on. Second, both groups were willing to use market intelligence to identify and target segments that were pro-Israel and who could influence public opinion and government policies towards Israel. Third, IINZ and AIJAC have used their communications output including websites, social media accounts, and print material to promote their products. Fourth, both groups have conducted campaigns in order to raise funds, influence public opinion, and lobby key stakeholders. Finally, both groups have used their communications output to promote their achievements and successes.

Segmentation, Targeting, and Positioning (STP)

This research found that all groups followed the three stages of Bartle and Griffith's (2002) segmentation, targeting, and positioning (STP) process. In terms of segmentation, two groups IINZ and APAN used public opinion polling, parliamentary transcripts, and petition campaigns to identify sympathetic civil society and political segments. While the other two groups PSNA and AIJAC did not disclose their segmentation practices, they conducted segmentation by identifying civil society, media, and political actors who were sympathetic to their cause and advocacy work.

In terms of targeting, all four organisations used their communications output and various relational activities including guest speaking engagements, information tours, public meetings, and fundraisers to reach out to these sympathetic civil society, media, and political actors. One general observation was the Palestinian solidarity groups targeted a left-wing and Arab-Muslim audience, while Zionist groups targeted a largely right-wing audience that included Jews, Christian Zionists, and conservative political parties.

In terms of positioning, all four groups conducted psychological positioning to convince their audiences of the righteousness and legitimacy of their causes. Palestinian solidarity groups framed the Palestinian struggle as one based on human rights, justice, and self-determination while presenting Israel as a racist, settler colonial state. By contrast, Zionist groups sought to present Israel's actions and policies towards the Palestinians as self-defence against aggression. Zionist groups also framed opposition towards Israel as based on anti-Semitism and anti-Zionism. In addition,

Israel was presented as the Jewish homeland while Zionism was framed as the expression of Jewish self-determination.

Internal Marketing

Drawing upon Pettitt's (2015) internal marketing framework, this research found that the four groups adopted base strategy by using ideological incentives to encourage activists and members to carry out external communications and relational activities. As cause groups, the groups designed their product and campaigns around the needs and expectations of their core supporters. Palestinian solidarity groups regarded advancing Palestinian rights and self-determination as their groups' core product, while Zionist groups regarded defending Israel and combating anti-Semitism as their core product. As a theory, the base strategy was useful for explaining how a cause-oriented group uses ideological commitment as the glue that binds together its support base.

Public Diplomacy and Nation Branding

The author's research found that the advocacy groups conducted various forms of public diplomacy and nation branding through their communications and advocacy work. Besides promoting their stated cause, these groups sought to help states and sub-national actors to manage their international image and occasionally to advance their perceived national interests and aspirations. First, this research found that three groups IINZ, AIJAC, and APAN had cultivated relations with foreign governments and their local representatives in Australia and New Zealand. AIJAC and the IINZ succeeded in cultivating relations with senior Israeli policy-makers and officials including Prime Minister Benjamin Netanyahu and Ambassador Itzhak Gerberg. While APAN had cultivated relations with the Palestinian Ambassador Abdulhadi and senior Palestinian Liberation Organisation (PLO) official Hanan Ashrawi, the PSNA appeared to have no direct contact and ties with the Palestinian Authority, which may reflect the Palestinian General Delegation's limited travel expenditure. While the PSNA lacked formal ties to the Palestinian Authority, it promoted pro-Palestinian messages, heritage, and supported the BDS movement through its communications output and advocacy activities. The higher level of interaction between pro-Israel groups and the Israeli Government in comparison to that between Palestinian solidarity groups and the Palestinian

Authority reflects the asymmetry of power and resources between Israel and the Palestinian Authority.

Second, all groups conducted image management and cultural heritage promotion through their communications output including websites, social media, print media, op-ed columns and letters, and media interviews. In general, pro-Israel groups sought to defend controversial Israeli policies and actions while highlighting favourable stories about Israel that they felt the media neglected. Meanwhile, pro-Palestinian groups sought to raise awareness of the Palestinian struggle and plight while documenting perceive Israeli aggression and human rights abuses. Different groups sought to portray their side as the victim and the other side as the aggressor. Cultural heritage promotion took the form of highlighting either Jewish or Palestinian culture, heritage, and history. Image management appeared to take precedence over cultural heritage promotion. Reflecting the asymmetry between Israel and the Palestinians, Zionist groups were more likely to engage in tourism promotion than Palestinian solidarity groups.

Third, all groups sponsored various relational activities including speaking engagements, public meetings, rallies, film festivals, and information trips with the goal of raising awareness and sympathy for the faction they were supporting. The groups sought to bring sympathetic guest speakers including government officials, civil society leaders, and activists to "educate" local audiences in New Zealand and Australia about the situation in Israel and the Palestinian Territories. Notable Palestinian solidarity guest speakers have included former Palestinian Prime Minister Salam Fayyad, Palestinian activists such as Ali Abunimah, Rafeef Ziadah, Huwaida Arraf, and Ramzy Baroud, dissident Israeli activists such as Gideon Levy and Jeff Halper, and the British musician Roger Waters. Meanwhile, notable pro-Israel guest speakers have included Israeli Ambassador to New Zealand Itzhak Gerbeg, retired Israeli politicians Einat Wilf, Tzachi Hanegbi, former Israeli military spokesperson Lt. Colonel Peter Lerner, Palestinian dissident Bassem Eid, and Middle East Forum founder and President Daniel Pipes. The presence of these speakers shows that the groups have worked with state actors and sympathetic civil society actors to advance public diplomacy and nation branding. Public meetings and rallies such as the "Celebrate Israel at 70" event in Auckland and the various BDS boycott campaigns were also used to express local solidarity and support for either Israel or the Palestinians within New Zealand and Australia. Film festivals such as the Waiheke Palestine Film Festival and the screening of the Israeli film *Ben Gurion: Epilogue* at the 13th Doc Edge festival were used to promote the Palestinian and Israeli narratives and film industries. Information trips were also used to educate New Zealand and Australian participants about the situation on the ground and help build relationships and networks with local political and civil society actors in Israel-Palestine.

Value of the Analytical Framework

Overall Findings

- In terms of marketing orientations, Palestinian solidarity groups favoured a product-orientation that placed their cause at the centre of their communications and advocacy work. By contrast, Zionist groups favoured a sales-orientation which involved using their communications output and advocacy work to sell their cause to the public and other influential actors.
- In terms of "segmentation, targeting, and positioning," all groups identified sympathetic segments and targeted them through their communications output and relational activities. All groups used psychological positioning to promote their cause in a favourable light while casting the opposing side in a negative light.
- In terms of internal marketing, all the groups pursued a base strategy where membership was motivated by ideological affinity for the Israeli or Palestinian causes. A base strategy occurs when leaders promote a product that resonates with an organisation's most committed supporters. This can include pursuing policies and rhetoric that reflect the group's ideological foundations. While Pettitt (2015) had political parties in mind when designing this strategy, it can also apply to advocacy groups. A base strategy is similar to a "dignified democracy" strategy, which uses solidarity incentives (the satisfaction of feeling part of an organisation through activism) to create its product through apparently democratic processes. While the Palestinian solidarity groups studied did use solidarity incentives to motivate their members and supporters, the research generated little insight into how they created their product by consulting with the membership. Hence, a base strategy provided a better explanation of how the groups used their cause and goals to motivate members and supporters. As cause groups, none of them used material incentives

to motivate their members. The empty vessel approach would also be at odds with the groups' commitment to shared set of beliefs and goals. The research also did not support the "effective democracy" strategy where the membership plays an important role in the creation and ownership of the product. Instead, the evidence supported a base strategy where the group's leadership designed a product that appealed to their core supporters.
- In terms of public diplomacy, all groups apart from the PSNA maintained some level of contact with states and non-state actors including diplomats and policy-makers. All four groups used their communications output to promote messages and arguments produced by the state or non-state actor whom they were supporting. They also used relational activities such as guest speaking engagements and information trips to promote managing the state actor or sub-national actor's international image and foster stronger relations. The Palestinian solidarity groups also voluntarily identified with the goals of the BDS movement, a transnational solidarity group.
- In terms of nation branding, the groups engaged in either cultural heritage or tourism promotion through their communications output and relational activities. On a communications level, they produced literature and media promoting the culture, heritage, and identity of the country and people they supported. On a relational level, they used public events such as guest speaking engagements, fundraisers, film festivals, and information trips for cultural and heritage promotion purposes. The author's research suggests that public diplomacy and nation branding overlap in several areas including public relations, tourism, cultural promotion, and informational trips. Reflecting the asymmetry between Israel and the Palestinians, the former was more likely to engage in tourism promotion.

Strengths

This research found that the synthesised analytical framework (Table 6.1) proved useful for analysing advocacy groups' political marketing, public diplomacy, and nation branding activities, focusing on four pro-Israel and pro-Palestinian advocacy groups in New Zealand and Australia. These strengths are outlined below:

- First, this framework analysed how groups marketed their causes to their local audiences in New Zealand and Australia through their communications output and relational activities.
- Second, this framework looked at how groups identified sympathetic segments, targeted them through a range of communications output and relational activities, and positioned their cause and messages to maximise their appeal.
- Third, this framework looked at how groups used their cause and ideology to mobilise their supporters and members.
- Fourth, this framework explored how these groups supported the public diplomacy and nation branding efforts of states and subnational actors through their communications output and advocacy activities. The research findings suggest that the groups functioned as independent allies rather than proxies of state actors.
- Despite its focus on pro-Israel and pro-Palestinian advocacy groups, this framework's criteria can be used to analyse a range of different advocacy groups in various settings, since it covers several key hallmarks of advocacy groups' work, namely their communications output, lobbying, public gatherings, recruitment/mobilisation, and networking activities and strategies.

Through these activities, groups sought to promote awareness and support for their causes while advancing the messages, goals, and interests of state actors and factions (namely Israel and the Palestinians).

Limitations

Though the content analysis and interviews addressed the research question, hypothesis, and analytical framework, there were still limitations in how the advocacy groups met the analytical framework's criteria, the availability of research participants, and differences between the content analysis and interview findings.

First, there were some limitations in how the advocacy groups met the criteria of the analytical framework:

- In terms of marketing orientation, this research suggests that advocacy groups are less likely to pursue a market-orientation since they are unwilling to let the market of public and elite opinion to dictate the identity and composition of their product.

- In terms of positioning, the groups studied appeared to prefer psychological positioning over "real positioning," which involves altering the product itself to cater market demands. This may not be reflective of all groups depending on the cause, organisation, and the issue at stake. The case studies preferred to change public perceptions of their cause. For example, Palestinian solidarity groups sought to present the Palestinians as fighting for human rights and self-determination, while Zionist groups sought to frame Israeli military actions as self-defence against terrorism.
- In terms of internal marketing, future research could explore how groups can design their programme in consultation with their members. While the research findings strongly suggested that the groups pursued a base strategy by promoting a product that resonated with their support base, an alternative hypothesis is that the groups pursued a dignified democracy strategy where they used solidarity incentives (the sense of being part of a cause group) to mobilise their members. This strategy would involve genuine consultation with the members. Since the author is not a member of these organisations or privy to their inner workings, this limited his ability to investigate the extent to which members had a role in designing the product. Future research could investigate this topic.
- The public diplomacy and nation branding angles may not be suitable for all groups and issues that do not involve state and subnational actors, foreign policy, and international relations.

Despite these limitations, the framework can be applied to other cause groups working on different cause issues including climate change, the environment, abortion, and LGBT rights. It can also be used to analyse groups taking diametrically opposed views and positions on these issues by focusing on how they market their causes.

Second, the author had trouble recruiting interviewees from AIJAC. The author had interviewed members of the organisations to corroborate the findings of the content analysis and fill gaps relating to their market intelligence, segmentation, targeting, and recruitment strategies and activities. While representatives from PSNA, IINZ, and APAN were willing to be interviewed, the author was unable to interview both current and former members of AIJAC, who declined to be interviewed. To address these gaps, the researcher consulted the works of Reich (2004), Rutland (2004), Levey and Mendes (2004), Loewenstein (2006), Han and Rane (2013), Lyons (2017), and Gawenda (2020), which gave useful insight into AIJAC's agenda and activities. Engaging with the prior literature on AIJAC helped inform this research about what areas have been covered as well as gaps that can be covered by this research.

Third, there were some differences between the content analysis and interview findings. While problematic, they also affirm the value of a multi-method approach since the researcher's observations may vary from those of practitioners from the case studies. While both Minto (personal communication, February 28, 2020) and Morrison (personal communication, April 7, 2020) claimed that their organisations did not conduct segmentation, the content analysis found that the PSNA and APAN practised some degree of segmentation. While the PSNA identified several sympathetic segments including the Arab-Muslim community, left-wing civil society groups and politicians, and dissident Jews for outreach, APAN used parliamentary transcripts and petition campaigns to identify sympathetic political allies. However, the content analysis generated little information about APAN's segmentation activities towards civil society and media actors; a gap which future research can address.

These variations between the content analysis and interview findings show that groups may be hesitant to disclose information about their segmentation strategies and practices into the public domain.

These three limitations did not affect the empirical findings of this research, which showed that the groups conducted political marketing, public diplomacy, and nation branding through their communications output and advocacy work.

Contributions to the Academic Literature

This research undertook a multi-field literature review of advocacy, public diplomacy, nation branding, and political marketing, as well as drawing on the international literature on Israeli and Palestinian groups. This literature search identified four major gaps. First, the New Zealand literature on Israel-Palestine has focused on bilateral relations and trade and devoted limited attention to advocacy groups. Second, while there was some limited research focusing on Jewish and Zionist groups in New Zealand, there was limited exploration of their political marketing, public diplomacy, and nation branding activities. Third, there was a smaller volume of literature focusing on the Australian Palestinian solidarity groups. Fourth, while the literature search identified a significant body of literature on

Israeli and Zionist political marketing, public diplomacy, and nation branding, there was limited corresponding literature on Palestinian political marketing, public diplomacy, and nation branding. While seeking to address these gaps, this research made four main contributions to the academic literature on advocacy, political marketing, public diplomacy, and nation branding: namely enriching the advocacy literature on both Zionist and Palestinian solidarity groups in New Zealand and Australia, showing that international advocacy groups, including pro-Israel and pro-Palestinian groups, can use political marketing, and exploring the role of non-state actors in carrying out both public diplomacy and nation branding. These are discussed below.

First, this research has enriched the advocacy literature on New Zealand and Australian-based groups working on Israel-Palestine issues by exploring their contributions to political marketing, public diplomacy, and nation branding. The research looked at three groups that had not been previously studied in substantial depth: the PSNA, IINZ, and APAN. While AIJAC has previously been studied by Reich (2004), Rutland (2004), and Han and Rane (2013), these early works did not analyse the political marketing, public diplomacy, and nation branding aspects of their advocacy work. Besides exploring how the groups promoted their cause and messages, recruited sympathetic segments and allies, and mobilised their support base, this research focused on how they sought to influence government, public, media, and civil society attitudes and policies towards Israel-Palestine through their communications output and advocacy network. In addition, this research also explored how these groups networked with other like-minded individuals, groups, and state actors in New Zealand and abroad; embedding them in cause-oriented transnational solidarity networks such as the BDS movement and the informal pro-Israel "transnational advocacy network." This research contributes to the academic literature on the BDS movement by showing how groups in New Zealand and Australia engage in boycott and divestment activities on both a local and international level. In short, this research not only enriches the international literature on groups interested in Israel-Palestine issues but also engages in boundary spanning by overlapping with the political marketing, public diplomacy, and nation branding sub-fields.

Second, this research explored how international advocacy groups, particularly Israeli and Palestinian advocacy groups, used political marketing strategies and techniques in their communications and advocacy activities, demonstrating that political marketing is used beyond parties not just domestically by advocacy groups or NGOs but also in international affairs. This research found that several political marketing theories and concepts including Lees-Marshment's (2004, 2014) product/sales/market-oriented framework, Bartle and Griffith's (2002) "segmenting, targeting, and positioning" process, and Pettitt's (2015) internal marketing framework were useful frameworks for analysing how the groups pitched their campaigns and activities, identified their supporters and reached out to them, and mobilised their members and supporters through ideological incentives. While Palestinian solidarity groups preferred product-oriented marketing, pro-Israel groups favoured sales-oriented marketing which included using market intelligence to sell their product. While pro-Palestinian groups tended to attract left-wing and Arab-Muslim segments, pro-Israel groups segments tended to attract Jewish, Christian Zionist, and right-wing segments. All four groups subscribed to a base strategy which involved appealing to their members and supporters' ideological commitment to advancing certain causes, whether it be defending Israel and combating anti-Semitism or advancing Palestinians rights and self-determination. In short, political marketing permeated their messaging, advocacy, and mobilisation strategies and activities, showing that marketing has a wider reach into political behaviour beyond its application to domestic candidates, parties, and elections.

Third, this research drew attention to the role of non-state actors such as advocacy groups in supporting Israeli and Palestinian public diplomacy efforts in Australia and New Zealand. Advocacy groups have contributed to public diplomacy by advancing the messages, arguments, and interest of state actors through their communicational output and relational activities including lobbying, mass gatherings, and informational trips. First, this research enriched the literature on Israeli public diplomacy by exploring the role of non-state actors in advancing public diplomacy in Australasia, with specific attention to IINZ and AIJAC. These groups promoted pro-Israel messages and arguments defending Israeli policies and actions and combating both real and perceived anti-Semitism and anti-Zionism through their communications output and literature. On a relational level, these groups also sponsored Israeli political, media, and civil society figures including Netanyahu and Gerbeg, film festivals and other cultural events, and information trips to Israel-Palestine. Second, this research also contributed to the limited literature on Palestinian public diplomacy by focusing on how the PSNA and APAN advanced Palestinian messages, goals, and interests through their communications output and advocacy work. While the links and connections between the Palestinian Authority and these two advocacy groups were looser compared to their Zionist counterparts, they supported many key Palestinian goals, such as advancing Palestinian rights, justice, and statehood; ending the Israeli military occupation, settlement expansion, and Separation Barrier; and holding Israel accountable for alleged human rights abuses and injustices. These goals and themes surfaced throughout their communications output and advocacy work. While the PSNA appeared not to have direct links to the Palestinian Authority, its Australian counterpart APAN had cultivated relations with some Palestinian officials and diplomats including Ambassador Abdulhadi, who attended several of their public events and fundraisers. The limited literature on Palestinian public diplomacy may reflect the asymmetry between Israel and the Palestinians. Taken together, this research shows that non-state actors can act as "force multipliers" in helping states to conduct their public diplomacy. Finally, this research also addressed the relationship between governments and non-state actors raised in Cull's (2009) New Public Diplomacy model by showing that the advocacy groups functioned primarily as independent actors with their own goals and interests rather than operating as foreign agents of state actors. While advocacy groups and state actors did work together when their goals and interests aligned, the former answered primarily to their own domestic leaderships and support bases rather than state actors. Though not all the groups studied had relations with state actors, these interactions gave them a sense of legitimacy and purpose among their members and supporters.

Fourth, this research contributed to the nation branding literature by showing how advocacy groups can engage in nation branding through their communications output and advocacy work. All four case studies used their communications output and advocacy activities such as print, online, and audio-visual media, speaking engagements, fundraisers, public gatherings, information trips, and politically oriented tourism to promote their causes and manage the image of the state or sub-national actor they were supporting. Reflecting the asymmetry between Israel and the Palestinians, pro-Israel groups conducted both tourism promotion and crisis management, while Palestinian solidarity groups tended to focus more on crisis management. In addition, this research also expanded upon Beirman's (2000) and Avraham's (2009) research into NGOs' involvement in facilitating politically oriented tourism (a subset of nation branding) to Israel-Palestine by exploring how Australian and New Zealand-based groups promoted tourism and information trips groups as a means of promoting their narratives about Israel-Palestine. Finally, this research found that there was an overlap between public diplomacy and nation branding since cultural heritage and tourism promotion activities were linked to the efforts of states and allied civil society actors to manage their international image. Given public diplomacy's broader, international focus, this research approached nation branding as a subset of public diplomacy.

In summary, this research has contributed to academic research by:

1. Expanding the literature on both pro-Israel and pro-Palestinian advocacy groups in New Zealand and Australia. It also expanded the limited literature on Palestinian solidarity groups in Australia while adding an Australasian dimension to the international literature on the BDS movement.
2. Demonstrating that political marketing can be used outside of domestic party politics and elections by a range of actors including international advocacy groups.
3. Showing that advocacy groups can support states' public diplomacy activities in a meaningful way while retaining their autonomy.
4. Showing that advocacy groups can engage in nation branding for both image management and tourism promotion purposes.

This research has shown that advocacy groups can conduct political marketing, public diplomacy, and nation branding: activities which had traditionally been conducted by states, political parties, and politicians. This demonstrates that branding and marketing are being used in politics by advocacy groups and other non-traditional actors in new ways with international aspects to its application.

Lessons for Practitioners

The conclusion will also have several lessons for practitioners in the areas of advocacy, political marketing, public diplomacy, and nation branding:

1. That advocacy groups can apply marketing methods and techniques such as market intelligence, internal marketing, segmentation, and targeting to communicating their message and recruiting people to their causes.

2. To get the message out, it is important to use a wide range of communications mediums (including print, online, social media platforms, and audio-visual content) and activities (such as meetings, guest speaking events, demonstrations, fundraisers, etc.) to make your presence felt in the public.
3. Market intelligence and segmentation can be used to reach certain demographics and groups. The message can be pitched differently without altering the original product depending on the audience. For example, both pro-Israel and pro-Palestinian advocates have sought to appeal to ethnic minorities by linking their cause to indigenous rights and self-determination.
4. It is important that advocacy groups have a clear product (i.e. set of goals and values) in order to recruit people to their group and cause.
5. It is advantageous that advocacy groups target key stakeholders including political elites, the media, and civil society leaders. Winning over political elites is key to influencing the public policy process, while influencing the media is key to influencing public opinion. Civil society leaders may be key to reaching certain ethnic, social, and faith segments.
6. That advocacy groups can work with state actors in areas of shared interests and value. Working with state actors can give them access to key policy-makers and resources. However, too overt a relationship can also tarnish the advocacy groups as "foreign agents." Thus, the relationship needs to be carefully managed.
7. That governments can harness the power of advocacy groups when engaging in public diplomacy. They can serve as force multipliers for influencing political elites, media coverage, and public opinion. However, an overtly visible relationship can also lead to accusations of foreign interference. Thus, the relationship needs to be carefully managed.

References

Avraham, E. (2009). Marketing and managing nation branding during prolonged crisis: The case of Israel. *Place Branding and Public Diplomacy, 5*(3), 202–212. https://doi.org/10.1057/pb.2009.15

Bartle, J., & Griffiths, D. (2002). Social-psychological, economic and marketing models of voting behaviour compared. In N. J. O'Shaughnessy & S. C. M. Henneberg (Eds.), *The idea of political marketing* (pp. 19–37). Praeger.

Beirman, D. (2000). Destination marketing: The marketing of Israel in Australia and the south-west Pacific. *Journal of Vacation Marketing*, 6(2), 145–153. https://doi.org/10.1057/pb.2009.15

Beirman, D. (2002). Marketing of tourism destinations during a prolonged crisis: Israel and the Middle East. *Journal of Vacation Marketing*, 8(2), 167–176.

Brin, E. (2006). Politically-oriented tourism in Jerusalem. *Tourist Studies*, 6(3), 215–243. https://doi.org/10.1177/1468797607076672

Campo, S., & Alvarez, M. D. (2014). Can tourism promotions influence a Country's negative image? An experimental study on Israel's image. *Current Issues in Tourism*, 17(3), 201–219. https://doi.org/10.1080/13683500.2013.766156

Cobb, R., & Elder, C. (1972). *Participation in American politics: The dynamics of agenda building*. John Hopkins University Press.

Cull, N. J. (2009). *Public diplomacy: Lessons from the past*. Figueroa Press.

Gawenda, M. (2020). *The power broker: Mark Leibler, an Australian Jewish life*. Monash University Press.

Gilboa, E. (2001). Diplomacy in the media age: Three models of uses and effects. *Diplomacy and Statecraft*, 12(2), 1–28. https://doi.org/10.1080/0959229010840620

Gilboa, E. (2008). Searching for a theory of public diplomacy. *The Annals of the American Academy*, 616(1), 55–77. https://doi.org/10.1177/0002716207312142

Han, E., & Rane, H. (2013). *Making Australian foreign policy on Israel-Palestine: Media coverage, public opinion and interest groups. Islamic studies series.* (Book 13). Melbourne University Press.

Keck, M. E., & Sikkink, K. (1998). *Activists beyond borders: Advocacy networks in international politics*. Cornell University Press.

Lang, G., & Lang, K. (1983). *The battle for public opinion: The president, the press and the polls during Watergate*. Columbia University Press.

Lees-Marshment, J. (2004). *The political marketing revolution: Transforming the government of the UK*. Manchester University Press.

Lees-Marshment, J. (2014). *Political marketing: Principles and applications* (2nd ed.). Routledge.

Levey, G. B., & Mendes, P. (2004). The Hanan Ashrawi affair: Australian Jewish politics on display. In G. B. Levey & P. Mendes (Eds.), *Jews and Australian politics* (pp. 215–230). Sussex Academic Press.

Loewenstein, A. (2006). *My Israel Question*. Melbourne University Press.

Lyons, J. (2017). *Balcony Over Jerusalem*. Harper Collins Publishers Australia.

Pettitt, R. T. (2015). Internal part political relationship marketing: Encouraging activism amongst local party members. In J. Lees-Marshment (Ed.), *Routledge handbook of political marketing* (pp. 137–150). Routledge.

Reich, C. (2004). Inside AIJAC – An Australian Jewish Lobby Group. In G. B. Levey & P. Mendes (Eds.), *Jews and Australian politics* (pp. 198–214). Sussex Academic Press.

Rutland, S. D. (2004). Who speaks for Australian Jewry. In G. B. Levey & P. Mendes (Eds.), *Jews and Australian politics* (pp. 29–43). Sussex Academic Press.

Szondi, G. (2008). *Public diplomacy and nation branding: Conceptual similarities and differences* (Discussion Papers in Diplomacy, Netherlands Institute of International Relations Cligendael, 2008). https://www.clingendael.nl/sites/default/files/20081022_pap_in_dip_nation_branding.pdf.

Zaharna, R. S. (2009). Mapping out a Spectrum of public diplomacy initiatives: Information and relational communication frameworks. In N. Snow & P. M. Taylor (Eds.), *Routledge handbook of public diplomacy* (pp. 86–99). Routledge.

Appendix

Websites

Palestine Solidarity Network Aotearoa (PSNA), https://www.psna.nz/
Israel Institute of New Zealand (IINZ), https://israelinstitute.nz
Australia/Israel and Jewish Affairs Council (AIJAC), https://aijac.org.au
Australia Palestine Advocacy Network, https://apan.org.au/

Print Media and Newsletters

Australia/Israel Review (*AIR*)
Pal News (APAN)
PSNA Newsletters, https://lettersforpalestine.weebly.com/psna-newsletters.html
The Advocate (IINZ)
Update on AIJAC

Social Media Accounts

Facebook

AIJAC, https://www.facebook.com/aijac.au

APAN, https://www.facebook.com/AustraliaPalestineAdvocacy Network/
IINZ, https://www.facebook.com/Israel.Institute.NZ/
PSNA, https://www.facebook.com/NZPalestine/

Instagram
AIJAC, https://www.instagram.com/aijac_update/?hl=en
APAN, https://www.instagram.com/apan4palestine/

Twitter
AIJAC, https://twitter.com/AIJAC_Update
APAN, https://twitter.com/apan4palestine
IINZ, https://twitter.com/IsraelInstNZ

Vimeo
APAN, https://vimeo.com/user42457739

YouTube
AIJAC, https://www.youtube.com/user/AIJACvideo
IINZ, https://www.youtube.com/channel/UCCunLRO6b9Z3JAlECtptLbQ
Palestine Human Rights Campaign's channel, https://www.youtube.com/user/palestinehumanrights/videos

Index

NUMBERS, AND SYMBOLS
2013 Australian federal election, 101–102
2016 Australian federal election, 103–104

A
ABC, *see* Australian Broadcasting Corporation
Abdulhadi, Izzat Salah, viii, 109
ACTU, *see* Australian Council of Trade Unions
AFOPA, *see* Australian Friends of Palestine Association
Ahed Tamimi, 22, 26, 27, 29, 106
AJC, *see* American Jewish Committee
AJDS, *see* Australian Jewish Democratic Society
Ali Abunimah, 34, 36, 112, 129
American Jewish Committee (AJC), 72, 80
Anti-Semitism, 7, 11, 24, 47, 48, 50, 52, 55, 56, 61, 62, 68, 69, 71, 72, 77–80, 87, 107, 122, 127, 128, 136
Anti-Zionism, 52, 80, 83, 87, 127, 136
Aotearoa-Israel Powhiri, 50, 53, 60
APHEDA, 111
Ashrawi, Hanan, 73, 106, 109, 128
Australian Broadcasting Corporation (ABC), 71, 73, 82, 110
Australian Council of Trade Unions (ACTU), 111
Australian federal election, 71
Australian Friends of Palestine Association (AFOPA), 112
Australian Greens/Greens, 72, 100, 104
Australian Jewish Democratic Society (AJDS), 72, 109
Australians for Palestine, 98

B

Baroud, Ramzy, 35, 36, 112, 129
Base strategy, 9, 32–34, 38, 54, 62, 79, 80, 87, 108, 109, 113, 128, 130, 133, 136
Bassem Eid, 83, 129
BDS, *see* Boycott, Divestment, and Sanctions
Bishop, Julie, 71
Boycott, Divestment, and Sanctions (BDS), 2, 4, 5, 23, 24, 27, 29–34, 38, 47, 48, 52, 53, 55, 56, 62, 71, 77, 78, 83, 84, 99, 102–104, 106, 107, 122, 125, 128, 129, 131, 135, 138
Browning, George, 98

C

Carolan, Joe, 28, 31
Carr, Bob, 73
Celebrate Israel at 70, 47, 50, 52, 59, 60, 129
C4Israel, *see* Christians for Israel New Zealand
Christians for Israel New Zealand (C4Israel), 50, 59
Christian Zionist, 25, 46, 50, 52, 59, 60
Coalition
   Liberal-National Coalition, 69–71, 101–103, 105
Coulton, Mark, 101
Cumin, David, viii, 11, 25, 26, 46, 59, 124

D

Danby, Michael, 71, 101
Davidson, Marama, 25, 28, 37, 53, 57
Dayenu
   Dayenu – NZ Jews Against the Occupation, 25, 27, 29

Delivery, 24, 47, 70, 99
Dreyfus, Mark, 71

E

ECAJ, *see* Executive Council of Australian Jewry
Executive Council of Australian Jewry (ECAJ), 71, 80, 104

F

Falk, Richard, 112
Fayyad, Salam, 106, 109, 112, 129
Fowler, Roger, viii, 25, 27, 31

G

Gaza March of Return/2018 Gaza March of Return, 58
Gaza Wars, 27, 35, 73
General Delegation/Palestinian General Delegation, 34, 109, 128
Gerbeg, Itzhak, 59, 60, 128, 129
Gillard, Julia, 85
Global Peace and Justice (GP&J), 22, 28
GP&J, *see* Global Peace and Justice
Green Party/ Green Party of Aotearoa New Zealand, 25, 26, 28–30

H

Halper, Jeff, 112, 129
Hanegbi, Tzachi, 83, 129
Huwaida Arraf, 26, 36, 129

I

IDF, *see* Israel Defense Forces
IHRA, *see* International Holocaust Remembrance Alliance

Indian Association, 50, 59
Internal marketing, 4, 7, 12, 32, 34, 38, 54, 62, 80, 87, 113, 124, 128, 130, 133, 136, 138
International Holocaust Remembrance Alliance (IHRA), 24
International Socialist Organisation, 26
Israel Defense Forces (IDF), 83
Israeli Committee Against House Demolitions, 111
Israeli Government, 5, 6, 55, 61, 63, 78, 81, 122, 125

J
Jones, Jeremy, 55, 85

K
Kaunds, Roy, 50, 59
Kia Ora Gaza, 22, 25, 28, 36, 37, 52

L
Labor Party
 Australian Labor Party, 70, 100, 103
Labour
 New Zealand Labour Party, 25, 26, 28, 49, 71, 110
Laundy, Craig, 101
Leibler, Mark, 81
Lerman, Eran, 83
Lerner, Peter, 83, 129
Levy, Gideon, 36, 112, 129
Liberal
 Liberal Party of Australia, 70, 71, 84, 101, 102, 104, 107
Lynch, Jake, 73
Lyons, John, 73, 105

M
Mahmoud Abbas, 77, 101
Marketing orientation, 7, 12, 23, 38, 48, 68, 98, 99, 113, 132
Market intelligence, 8, 46, 48, 49, 68, 86, 127, 133, 136, 138
McNeill, Sophie, 73
MEF, *see* Middle East Forum
Middle East Forum (MEF), 83, 129
Minto, John, viii, 11, 22, 23, 28, 29, 124
Morrison, Jessica, viii, 11, 124
Moses, Juliet, viii, 25, 26

N
Nasser Mashni, 98
National Party of Australia (NPA), 101
Nation State law
 2018 Nation State law, 70
Netanyahu, Benjamin, 3, 81, 128
New Zealand National Party (NZ National Party), 50
New Zealand Super Fund (NZ Super Fund), 27, 31
Ngaro, Alfred, 50, 52, 59
Nick Xenophon Team, 101, 103, 104
NPA, *see* National Party of Australia

O
Olive Kids, 98
One Nation, 69, 71, 74, 101

P
Palestine Human Rights Campaign (PHRC), 22, 29
Palestinian Authority
 Palestinian National Authority, 3, 5, 34, 37, 39, 58, 77, 83, 109, 122, 125, 128–129, 137

Palestinian Liberation Organisation (PLO), 58, 73, 128
Palestinian solidarity, 2–4, 6, 10, 21, 23–25, 27, 28, 31, 32, 35, 36, 49, 51–53, 59, 98, 102, 107, 112, 122, 123, 125–131, 133, 134, 136–138
Palestinian Women's Humanitarian Organisation, 111
Parke, Melissa, 100, 102
PHRC, *see* Palestine Human Rights Campaign
Pipes, Daniel, 83, 129
Plibersek, Tania, 71
PLO, *see* Palestinian Liberation Organisation
Positioning, 4, 7, 8, 23–32, 38, 48–54, 62, 70–79, 87, 100–108, 113, 123, 124, 126–128, 130, 133, 136
Product design, 24, 47, 69
Product-oriented, 22–24, 38, 98, 99, 113, 126, 136

R
Ramban Israel Fellowship, 69, 74, 81, 83, 84
Resolution 2334
  UN Security Council Resolution 2334, 3, 24, 46, 48, 49, 60
Rubenstein, Colin, 3, 70, 72, 76–78, 80, 82, 84

S
Sachs, Justine, 26, 27
Sales-oriented, 46–48, 54, 62, 68–70, 86, 126, 127, 136
SBS, *see* Special Broadcasting Service

Segmentation/ segmenting, 4, 7, 23, 32, 38, 46–50, 53, 62, 69, 70, 74, 87, 100, 101, 103, 107, 108, 113, 124, 127, 130, 133, 134, 138, 139
Shorten, Bill, 71, 85
SJP, *see* Students for Justice in Palestine
Slezak, Peter, 104
Socialist Alliance, 103, 104
Special Broadcasting Service (SBS), 70, 82, 85, 110
Students for Justice in Palestine (SJP), 1–2, 22, 33

T
Targeting/target, 4, 7, 8, 23–32, 38, 48–54, 62, 70–79, 87, 100–108, 123, 124, 126–128, 130, 133, 136, 138
Trotter, Perry, 46, 55
Trotter, Sheree, 52, 56
Turnbull, Malcolm, 71, 81

U
UNESCO, *see* United Nations Educational, Scientific and Cultural Organization
United Nations, 3, 52, 71, 77, 101, 103, 110, 112
United Nations Educational, Scientific and Cultural Organization (UNESCO), 71
United Nations Security Council, 3

V
Vamvakinou, Maria, 100
Visitor programme, 74, 81, 83, 86

W
Wakim, Janfrie, viii, 27, 30, 31
Waters, Roger, 112, 129
Wellington Palestine Group (WPG), 27
Wilf, Einat, 55, 83, 129
WPG, *see* Wellington Palestine Group

X
Xenophon, Nick, 101, 104

Z
Ziadah, Rafeef, 25, 36, 112, 129
Zionist/Zionism, 2–4, 7, 10, 26, 32, 36, 50, 52, 54, 55, 59–63, 71, 72, 78, 122, 125, 127–130, 133–137

GPSR Compliance
The European Union's (EU) General Product Safety Regulation (GPSR) is a set of rules that requires consumer products to be safe and our obligations to ensure this.

If you have any concerns about our products, you can contact us on

ProductSafety@springernature.com

In case Publisher is established outside the EU, the EU authorized representative is:

Springer Nature Customer Service Center GmbH
Europaplatz 3
69115 Heidelberg, Germany

www.ingramcontent.com/pod-product-compliance
Ingram Content Group UK Ltd.
Pitfield, Milton Keynes, MK11 3LW, UK
UKHW021251180426
11946UKWH00004B/82